MARIO PANSERA
AND JAVIER LLOVERAS

POST GROWTH INNOVATION

Resisting the Pursuit of Endless
Economic Growth

First published in Great Britain in 2026 by

Bristol University Press
University of Bristol
1-9 Old Park Hill
Bristol
BS2 8BB
UK
t: +44 (0)117 374 6645
e: bup-info@bristol.ac.uk

Details of international sales and distribution partners are available at bristoluniversitypress.co.uk

© Mario Pansera and Javier Lloveras 2026

The digital PDF and ePub versions of this title are available open access and distributed under the terms of the Creative Commons Attribution-NonCommercial-NoDerivatives 4.0 International licence (https://creativecommons.org/licenses/by-nc-nd/4.0/) which permits reproduction and distribution for non-commercial use without further permission provided the original work is attributed.

DOI: 10.51952/9781529249965

British Library Cataloguing in Publication Data
A catalogue record for this book is available from the British Library

ISBN 978-1-5292-4994-1 paperback
ISBN 978-1-5292-4995-8 ePub
ISBN 978-1-5292-4996-5 OA PDF

The right of Mario Pansera and Javier Lloveras to be identified as authors of this work has been asserted by them in accordance with the Copyright, Designs and Patents Act 1988.

All rights reserved: no part of this publication may be reproduced, stored in a retrieval system, or transmitted in any form or by any means, electronic, mechanical, photocopying, recording, or otherwise without the prior permission of Bristol University Press.

Every reasonable effort has been made to obtain permission to reproduce copyrighted material. If, however, anyone knows of an oversight, please contact the publisher.

The statements and opinions contained within this publication are solely those of the authors and not of the University of Bristol or Bristol University Press. The University of Bristol and Bristol University Press disclaim responsibility for any injury to persons or property resulting from any material published in this publication.

Bristol University Press works to counter discrimination on grounds of gender, race, disability, age and sexuality.

Cover design: blu inc
Front cover image: Artwork by Rebeca Arredondo
Bristol University Press uses environmentally responsible print partners.
Printed and bound in Great Britain by CPI Group (UK) Ltd,
Croydon, CR0 4YY

Bristol University Press' authorised representative in the
European Union is: Easy Access System Europe,
Mustamäe tee 50, 10621 Tallinn, Estonia,
Email: gpsr.requests@easproject.com

To Lola, Matteo, Mar, Emma, and all the other beings who make our lives worthwhile

Contents

Acknowledgements		vi
Introduction: What Do You Believe? A Miracle of Technology or Politics?		1
one	The Growth Delusion: How Innovation Fuels Our Path to Disaster	13
two	What's Wrong With Innovation and Why it Matters for a Post Growth Society	32
three	Caring and Maintaining	49
four	Organizations and Institutions for Post Growth	67
five	The Infrastructural Conditions of Post Growth	88
six	What Does it Mean Today to Democratize Technology?	111
Coda: Why Did We Stop Making Experiments?		134
Notes		139
References		147
Index		163

Acknowledgements

The research for this book was funded by a Starting European Research Council grant, 'PROSPERA: Prospering without growth: Science, Technology and Innovation in a post-growth era' (GA: 947713), The Ramón y Cajal programme [Grant RYC2021-034823-I funded by Spanish Ministry of Science and the European Union NextGeneration EU/PRTR] and the UE Horizon MSCA Individual Fellowships (GA 101066896).

This book is the result of five years of ongoing conversations, reflections, and collaborations with many friends and colleagues. We are especially grateful to Adrian Smith, Andrea Jiménez, Andrea Genovese, Mariano Fressoli, Aviram Sharma, Poonam Pandey, Tess Doezema, Stefania Barca, Samer Abdelnour, Yoshihiro Nakano, and numerous others in the degrowth community, whose insights and encouragement have greatly enriched our thinking. We would also like to thank the anonymous reviewers of the book proposal and manuscript for their thoughtful and constructive feedback. Finally, our sincere thanks go to the team at Bristol University Press for their support throughout the production and marketing process.

Introduction: What Do You Believe? A Miracle of Technology or Politics?

Imagine an architect presenting plans for a skyscraper without elevators, confidently arguing that by the time construction is complete, we will have flying vehicles to access the upper floors. Or picture a doctor advising you to continue smoking cigarettes and binge drinking on weekends, assuring you that cancer and cardiovascular diseases will soon be eradicated thanks to upcoming miraculous medical breakthroughs. You would almost certainly dismiss these individuals as reckless or delusional. And yet, this is precisely the kind of logic we collectively embrace when it comes to technological innovation as the dominant framework for addressing climate breakdown and ecological collapse. We place blind faith in future technologies to miraculously 'fix' the crises we face, ignoring the urgency of the present and the need for systemic change. This pervasive and often irrational reliance on technological progress sidesteps the uncomfortable reality that our current trajectory – rooted in overconsumption and unsustainable practices – demands immediate and transformative action, not speculative promises of future inventions.

In the pursuit of solutions to environmental degradation and resource depletion, an urgent and contentious debate has emerged among scientists, policy makers, and environmental activists. At its core, this debate centres on the viability of addressing ecological decline through technological innovation or systemic transformation. While the scientific community largely agrees on the critical necessity of reducing greenhouse gas emissions and redistributing resources to mitigate the worst impacts of climate change, there remains significant discord regarding the socio-political means best suited to achieving this objective. There are two prevailing paradigms that shape this discourse: the green growth model, often associated with eco-modernism, and its counterpoint post growth,[1] involving the critique of economic growth as inherently unsustainable.

Proponents of green growth argue for a paradigm that integrates economic and environmental objectives, positing that technological innovation can enable societies to 'decouple' economic growth from resource consumption and emissions. Central to this perspective is the belief that advances in clean technology, efficiency improvements, and renewable energy can allow for continued economic expansion without exacerbating ecological harm. The eco-modernist position,[2] which aligns closely with this vision, suggests that humanity can use science and technology to reconfigure industrial production, transport, and agricultural processes, leading to an era in which prosperity and ecological stability coexist (Asafu-Adjaye et al, 2015). This viewpoint maintains that economic growth is not only compatible with environmental sustainability but also essential to achieving it, as technological progress and wealth generation can provide the resources and incentives necessary for large-scale environmental solutions.

Yet, this approach has been met with increasing scepticism from a segment of the scientific and activist communities, who argue that the very pursuit of perpetual economic growth is the fundamental driver of environmental degradation (Kallis, 2021). From this perspective, the societal and economic structures that prioritize growth inherently lead to resource depletion and ecological imbalance. These critics of growth contend that technological innovations, while valuable, are insufficient to counteract the environmental impacts of a growth-oriented system. They argue that efforts to decouple growth from ecological impact tend to be offset by increased consumption elsewhere, a phenomenon often referred to as the 'rebound effect' (Parrique et al, 2019). Accordingly, they advocate for an alternative vision of sustainability that involves not merely the greening of growth but a fundamental shift away from growth itself, rethinking economic success in terms of human and ecological well-being rather than perpetual GDP expansion.

In this book, we fully embrace the post growth position. The only viable path to addressing the immense challenges humanity will face in the coming decades is through a democratic and carefully planned downscaling of economic activities in affluent, overconsuming economies to levels that are compatible with the planet's ecological limits. This deliberate reduction, often referred to by the provocative term 'degrowth', should primarily target the wealthiest nations and the richest 1 per cent of the global population. However, degrowth does not imply a blanket reduction across all sectors of the economy neither a relegation of the Global South into a state of under consumption. Certain areas both in the North and in the South, such as public health, caregiving, and renewable energy, urgently require expansion to meet societal needs and ensure well-being. On the other hand, industries like fossil fuels, military spending, and unsustainable polluting chemical production must be drastically scaled down or eliminated altogether. This implies a vision of a global constellation of a plurality of societies that are free from colonial bonds and that value balance and coexistence rather than unchecked growth and endless consumption.

At this point is important to notice that throughout this book, we often use the terms 'degrowth' and 'post growth' interchangeably. We are aware that these terms – and others in the wider semantic constellation, such as a-growth, doughnut economics, well-being economy, post-development, and prosperity without growth – have distinct genealogies, conceptual nuances, and political orientations (see Savini, 2024; Kallis et al, 2025). However, we also believe that the differences among them are often overstated, drifting into unproductive hair-splitting and artificial boundary-making. Our position aligns with the idea of degrowth as an umbrella concept (Kallis, 2011), or even a political slogan with theoretical implications (Latouche, 2009), which connects a family of post growth imaginaries and proposals. In this spirit, and building on our own work, we understand degrowth not as a monolithic theory, but as a plural, evolving, and contested space of thinking and practice – what we elsewhere call its ontological politics. From this perspective, the distinction between degrowth and post growth is less about clear-cut paradigmatic divergence and more about emphasis, tone, and context. Both refer to the search for viable alternatives to growth-dependent systems, and both contribute to a shared political and intellectual project: making a just, ecological, and democratic transition beyond growth.

But yet in proposing a beyond growth society, we are confronted with what we can call a *dual infeasibility*, which emerges as a critical concept for understanding the constraints faced by both camps. Dual infeasibility highlights the inherent impracticalities that hinder the respective implementation of both green growth and growth-critical approaches. On one hand, green growth strategies face challenges in achieving absolute decoupling rates and eco-efficiency improvements that have no precedent in human history, if we are to counteract the current trajectory of climate change. Research in this area shows that, at current rates, eco-efficiency improvements would need to increase *a tenfold* by 2025 to meet current climate targets while sustaining economic growth (Vogel and Hickel, 2023), something that at the time we are writing has clearly not happened. On the other hand, the proposal to abandon economic growth as a goal encounters significant socio-political resistance, given the extent to which contemporary societies and institutions are structured around growth-oriented metrics and imaginaries of success. Therefore, while advocates of green growth rely on nothing short of a technological miracle to achieve decoupling rates that are compatible with scientifically sound climate targets,

INTRODUCTION

degrowthers depend on a sort of political miracle for mass consumer societies to voluntarily embrace degrowth. In this sense, dual infeasibility underscores the paradox in which both pathways – despite their diametric opposition – encounter obstacles that prevent them from offering a fully viable solution to the ecological crisis.

With a specific emphasis on the role of the notion of technology and innovation in our societies, in this book we seek to unravel the complexities of this dichotomy. But before anything else, we need to face the fact that the conflict between growth and sustainability can't simply be solved by relying on technical development. The core argument of this book is that technical innovation isn't neutral or inevitable; it's a social process shaped by specific values and goals. More often than not, those values are set by powerful elites who prioritize their own interests. Over time, these values become so deeply embedded in society that we stop questioning them and treat them as common sense. Take climate change, for example. Instead of addressing the root causes, we see increasingly far-fetched solutions like geoengineering – huge, futuristic projects designed to manipulate the environment to 'fix' the crisis – or fairy tales with improbable technical feasibility, such as net-zero initiatives. These ideas often get a warm welcome, especially from techno-enthusiasts, because they promise to deliver economic growth and jobs while offering a shortcut to saving the planet. It's a lot like the movie *Don't Look Up*, where the main female character returns to her hometown only to find that her own mother supports drilling into the asteroid hurtling towards Earth. Why? Because extracting its precious minerals will create jobs, stimulate the economy, and – oh, by the way – save humanity in the process. The scene highlights the absurdity of prioritizing economic growth over genuine solutions to climate change, yet this mindset is everywhere. We've become so attached to growth that even when facing existential threats, we'd rather gamble on improbable, high-tech fixes than question the system that got us here in the first place.

We also should admit that growth's hegemony remains untouched in the face of mounting scientific evidence, in part because it aligns with ordinary people's desires and collective aspirations for rising living standards, typically measured through ever higher incomes and purchasing power. As Soper (2020) argues, a post growth transition would require nothing less than a 'cultural revolution'; that is, the emergence of a radically different value-orientation driven by revised conceptions of progress, prosperity, development, and the good life. And additionally, we might add, new imaginaries of science, technology and innovation are desperately needed. Imaginaries that in our opinion should be built around the notions of radical democracy and social control of technology.

These ideas are not totally new. Concepts such as socially useful production, appropriate technologies or convivial tools emerged in the 1970s in combination with the debates about the *Limits to Growth* and the work of early degrowth promoters like Ivan Illich, André Gorz, or Fritz Schumacher. What is new today is the pervasive presence of technology in our lives, its higher impact in reshaping social relations and its dramatic environmental cost. Moreover, as the recent call of the EU to rearm exemplifies, the growth imperative is further entrenched by the reciprocal interaction of political–economic structures, geopolitical relations, and militarization, each of which operates in complex and multidimensional ways. Albert (2024), for example, highlights how notions of national security and the framing of military spending as a means to stay safe in the context of increasing geopolitical instability plays a crucial role in maintaining this growth paradigm. For a nation to renounce growth is viewed as tantamount to a unilateral disarmament, especially given that economic growth underpins the military–industrial complex and drives the ever-increasing budgets needed to stay competitive in the global race for increasingly effective warfare technologies and innovations. Importantly, different technological systems can overcome what specific social groups may perceive as insurmountable limits – much like historical examples, such as the abolition of child labour, reveal the possibilities for systemic transformation. Recognizing these dynamics requires us to question not only how limits are framed but also the structures and ideologies that sustain growth hegemony.

Finally, some argue that things are even more complicated than that. Bentley Allan (2018) suggests that growth hegemony lies in the *cosmology of progress*, where economic growth is equated with, or at least seen as necessary for, the forward march of civilization. This cosmology is arguably the deepest and most enduring layer of growth ideology, as it speaks directly to existential and libidinal fears of both individual and collective mortality. Growth, in this sense, is not simply an economic imperative but a source of ultimate meaning and value – a response to humanity's deep-seated anxieties about death, insignificance, and impermanence. Grand civilizational projects rooted in expansion and development promise a form of immortality, symbolizing the persistence of human achievement far beyond the finite span of individual lives. This existential dimension lends growth a mythical or even religious quality, as many commentators have observed.[3] The allure of growth thus operates in ways that transcend rational argumentation, feeding into deeply ingrained narratives about humanity's place in the cosmos and its desire for mastery over the earth. Such attachments help explain the seemingly irrational persistence of growth commitments despite their ecological and social destructiveness. Challenging this hegemony, therefore, demands far more than technical solutions or economic critique; it requires a profound cultural and existential reorientation. Alternatives to growth must point towards new sources of meaning and value – ones grounded not in domination, expansion, or the promise of endless progress, but in reconnection with the earth, the rhythms of life, and a cosmos that is not ours to conquer but to dwell within. As Allan (2018) suggests, the post growth future must provide a new orientation that reconciles humanity with limits, offering ways of being that honour our finite existence while opening up deeper, more life-affirming possibilities for collective meaning and purpose.

Although we agree with the core Allan's argument, we still think that our fixation with economic growth is also an epiphenomenon linked to what Mark Fisher has called 'capitalist realism'. Mark Fisher (2009) coined the notion of capitalist realism to describe the pervasive narrative that capitalism is the only viable economic and social system, making it difficult to imagine or aspire to alternative ways of organizing society. Similarly, the contemporary debate about building a sustainable and prosperous future is held hostage by a pervasive growth realism – the belief that there is no alternative to the relentless pursuit of economic growth. Unlike overtly celebratory views in the past, some varieties of growth realism take a pragmatic and somewhat deflationary view which is explicitly anti-utopian. For instance, business leaders and policy makers increasingly promote growth as an effort to avoid falling behind rather than as a means to improve the present condition (Rosa, 2019). No matter how much growth is achieved, next year commands even more.

In growth realist terms, science, technology, and innovation discourses sustain the belief that growth is non-negotiable. It employs the language of mission-oriented innovation, sustainable development goals, green technological innovation or Circular Economy to sidestep the deeper issue – that continuous economic growth may be fundamentally incompatible with ecological limits. By promoting 'the right' growth, in the right form, with a right combination of eco-friendly product lines, sustainable technology, green certifications, and cause-driven branding, growth realism suggests that ecological challenges are solvable within the current system. Through the prism of growth realism, proposals by critical scholars and practitioners deviating from the growth pathway are often viewed as utopian, idealists, moralists, or doomsayers, while growth realism is upheld by self-proclaimed green technology pragmatists and real-world problem solvers. This realism allows growth to persist as a pragmatic necessity for a *green marketing*, even as environmental crises escalate (Lloveras et al, 2022).

Yet, the cracks and fissures in growth realism are amplified by the looming ecological crises we are recklessly accelerating towards. These fractures are not only intellectual; they often strike at something deeper, emotional and existential. This is evident when, as educators, we encounter the inevitable student question: 'Do you think we're going to be okay?' This emotional angst and sense of unease reflect the contradictions at the heart of growth realism – a growing discomfort with the overwhelming evidence of climate change, species loss, microplastic pollution, and other crises so vast they defy easy solutions. As sustainability researchers, we, too, grapple with these unsettling emotions. The source of this helplessness lies in the immense disconnect between the scale of the crisis and the superficial 'green' solutions growth realism offers – little more than green consumerism and incremental technological fixes – which only deepens the sense of futility. These solutions don't just fail to resolve the crisis – they exist to keep the machine running, no matter the cost.

In a way, growth realism persists, not because we truly believe it, but because the alternative terrifies us (Zizek, 2011). However, more and more people are beginning to recognize that the green promises of growth realism ring hollow. The public is increasingly aware that growth realism is an ideological 'straight jacket', suffocating our imagination and unnecessarily limiting our search for solutions. While we may still cling to growth realism out of fear, scepticism towards its sustainability is rising – emerging not just among students and academics but also in institutions like the European Parliament and within the business community.[4]

Degrowth and post growth thinking can tap into these cracks, offering an antidote to growth realism that prevents environmental anxieties from solidifying into cynicism or apathy. Rather than isolating these feelings in the private sphere of the individual, post growth thinking identifies their structural causes, channelling them into collective action and fostering a shared sense of possibility. Perhaps the apocalypse has already started. Perhaps we can still cancel the apocalypse. But to truly break free from growth realism, post growth thinking must offer hope without succumbing to the overly optimistic or comforting narratives typical of ecomodernism. In this regard, we align post growth with Moellendorf's (2022) assertion that 'hope does not require optimism'.

In the following pages of this book, we explore how the concept of technological innovation has become a central pillar in what can be described as the 'religion of economic growth'. We examine this dynamic through the lens of post growth perspectives, challenging the prevailing assumption in economics and policy making that innovation and growth are and must be inherently linked. At the same time, we critically engage with some of the existing post growth narratives, which often adopt a reductive low-tech stance that fails to capture the complexity and diversity of innovation. By bridging science and technology studies with contemporary post growth debates, this book aims to offer a timely and nuanced analysis of the challenges facing science, technology, and innovation as we navigate the transition beyond the paradigm of perpetual growth.

Overview of the book

In the next chapters we are going to explore how growth realism is constantly reproduced in our societies by heavily relying on unconditional faith in technology development and innovation. We do this by combining critiques coming from science technology and society studies with the rich tradition of critical studies on technology that inspired contemporary degrowth and, more recently, post growth scholarship. Chapter 1 traces the historical transformation of innovation from a term associated with corruption to an unquestioned economic imperative. Post-World War II techno-optimism,

INTRODUCTION

influenced by figures like Schumpeter, cemented innovation as the engine of growth, ignoring ecological and social costs. Despite warnings like the *Limits to Growth*, institutions such as the Organisation for Economic Co-operation and Development (OECD) rebranded growth-centric innovation as 'sustainable development' while obscuring its colonial and extractive foundations. Case studies – from artificial intelligence (AI)-driven warfare in Gaza to coltan mining in the Congo – reveal how modern innovation perpetuates old colonial processes enabled by contemporary technology such as ecocide, epistemicide, and genocide. The chapter argues that systemic change is necessary to decouple progress from growth, prioritizing ecological and social justice over profit-driven expansion.

Since the 1970s, critics like Bookchin, Gorz, Schumacher, and Illich have challenged mainstream technological development, advocating for tools that foster autonomy, sustainability, and decentralization. Illich's 'convivial technologies', for instance, emphasize user empowerment and ecological regeneration. Chapter 2 dismantles three key growth-paradigm assumptions: technological determinism (the belief that technology evolves autonomously, dictating societal change), productivism (the idea that innovation inherently drives prosperity), and the illusion of control (the conviction that we can always manage the negative consequences of technology). Instead, it argues that technology reflects social power structures and often exacerbates inequality. By rejecting these assumptions, a post growth framework can redirect innovation towards justice and sustainability.

Moving beyond Schumpeter's creative destruction, Chapter 3 proposes an innovation model rooted in care, repair, and democratic participation. Drawing on research into makerspaces, fab labs, and right-to-repair movements, it highlights how users – not just corporations – can shape technological development. These grassroots initiatives demonstrate that innovation need not be exploitative but can instead prioritize durability, accessibility, and community resilience. The chapter calls for a shift from market-driven disruption to regenerative and socially embedded technological practices.

Based on empirical research from the European Research Council–funded PROSPERA project, Chapter 4 examines real-world examples of post growth production models. From cooperative enterprises to open-source platforms, these cases illustrate how economic activity can thrive without growth dependency. The chapter explores how institutions – whether local governments, worker-owned firms, or commons-based initiatives – can restructure innovation around equity and sustainability. By decentralizing control and redefining value beyond GDP, these models offer pathways towards a post growth future.

Early degrowth discourse often idealized small-scale, low-tech solutions, but contemporary debates have started engaging also with complex systems and large technological systems. Chapter 5 navigates the tension between infrastructure expansion and ecological limits, advocating for strategic scaling: expanding high-tech solutions where they reduce carbon footprints while phasing out destructive industries. Crucially, it argues for democratic governance of infrastructures, ensuring that their development aligns with sustainability and equity rather than corporate profit.

Finally, Chapter 6 explores what it means to democratize technological development, reviewing past attempts and present experiments in participatory governance. From citizen-led energy cooperatives to open-source software movements, it assesses successes and failures in making technology accountable to communities. The book concludes by reimagining innovation beyond growth – centring creativity, experimentation, and collective imagination as the true drivers of human progress. A post growth world, it argues, must disentangle innovation from exploitation, fostering systems that serve people and the planet rather than endless expansion.

ONE

The Growth Delusion: How Innovation Fuels Our Path to Disaster

In a world that feels increasingly chaotic and unsafe, Donald Trump's re-election has created ripples of reaction across the Atlantic. To his supporters and various right-wing movements worldwide, it serves as both a reinforcement of their ideology and an encouragement to persist in opposing progressive agendas, including feminism, multiculturalism, social justice initiatives, climate change mitigation, and progressive woke culture. For many others – especially Democrats and the so-called liberal voices – it feels like the end of the road, a collapse of ideals; a descent into despair. In Spain, while we are writing, on the streets of Valencia the muddy aftermath of unprecedented floods tells a story of a climate in rebellion, a world where nature's fury meets human indifference. Volunteers sift through piles of cars looking for bodies as families mourn lives lost to a catastrophe that scientists have warned about for months. Across the Atlantic, the rhetoric is strikingly detached from this chaos. Keir Starmer,[1] the UK Prime Minister, raises his glass to 'growth and security' and the enduring UK-US partnership. 'Innovation and economic growth', he declares, will keep both nations thriving for years to come. But what of the children torn apart in Gaza, victims of a genocide and ethnic cleansing that started in 1948 and that has no end in sight? What of the daily horrors in

Ukraine, where fields and cities alike are battlefields, and hope feels as fragile as the icy winters that descend there? What of the hilly north Kivu of Congo where armed conflicts over precious minerals – like coltan, which fuels our hunger for microchips – are masked as ethnic violence? The world's crises are staggering in their complexity and relentless in their brutality, yet they seem to orbit around one unwavering mantra: economic growth.

Growth, a simple word, yet so all-encompassing. It's been the North Star of late-stage capitalism, a guiding principle whose importance dwarfs all else (Pfotenhauer et al, 2022). In the halls of power, decisions are not shaped by the bodies buried under Valencian mud or the shattered lives in Palestine. Instead, they are driven by GDP figures, stock market highs, and the next big technological innovation – each feeding the other. It's a mad cycle: growth demands innovation, innovation demands growth, and the wheel spins faster, without rest, without reflection, without breaks. The command is clear, as sociologist Hartmunt Rosa (2019) put it: 'Run, run always faster, not to reach an objective, but to maintain the *status quo*, to simply remain in the same place'. The system devours itself, endlessly, while the world burns and society breaks.

The term 'technological somnambulism', coined by Langdon Winner (2004), comes to mind – a sleepwalking society, intoxicated by the allure of progress but oblivious to its consequences. There's a paradox here that borders on the absurd. The world is burning, flooding, and bleeding, yet the focus remains fixed on scaling up, innovating more, producing more, and moving faster. Innovation is heralded as the panacea for all ills, as if a shiny new app or a clever AI algorithm might miraculously halt the rising seas or bring peace to war-torn regions. The belief in growth is so ingrained that questioning it feels almost heretical. Why slow down when you can accelerate? Why stop and reflect when we can innovate?

How the obsession with innovation and the pursuit of growth became inseparable

Yet in the sixteenth and seventeenth centuries, the rejection or removal of 'innovations' was often a leitmotif tied to the idea of returning to 'purity', as innovation was largely synonymous with corruption (Godin, 2023). In seventeenth-century England, the term 'innovation' was not directly linked with technology but indicated any form of novelty. The word emerged as something to oppose and was employed by both conformists and dissenters for various political and religious purposes. It served two main functions: first, as an injunction against change, and second, as a tool to accuse and delegitimize non-conformists. While terms such as 're-form', 're-generate', and 're-new' were associated with positive connotations of improvement, innovation was equated with negative ideas, such as 'alteration', 'corruption', and 'pollution'.

The fate of the meaning of the word 'innovation' drastically changed during the first industrial revolution. From signalling moral corruption to becoming a synonym for progress and a beacon of hope, how we got trapped into the rhetoric of innovation is historically intimately related with our current obsession with economic growth. The idea of growth is certainly intertwined with narrative of progress and enlightenment and has been since the very beginning of the industrial era (Latouche, 2009; Sachs, 2010). Nevertheless, the notion that societies require unending economic growth for prosperity originates from the post-World War II period (Rist, 2011). This era was marked by unprecedented advancements in science and technology, which introduced a constant stream of products, services, and novel materials that captured the collective imagination. Such was the momentum of technological optimism that individuals in the 1950s anticipated a near future of flying cars and other fabulous artefacts (Graeber, 2012).

This is also the era in which the concept of technological innovation becomes formalized and enters the academic debate about development and economic growth. Joseph Schumpeter, the Austrian naturalized American economist who is considered the father of innovation studies, was among the first scholars to highlight the transformative role of technological change in the 1930s, identifying it as the primary driver of capitalist expansion. He demonstrated that technological innovation continuously revolutionizes production and delivery processes, injecting both dynamism and instability into competitive markets. According to Schumpeter, the capacity to innovate – defined as the ability to harness technological change for market advantage – is embedded within individuals and organizations and is the first source of growth. He originally identified the visionary entrepreneur as the primary agent of innovation, someone perpetually seeking competitive advantage. Later, however, Schumpeter revised this position in light of post-war developments, observing that the research and development departments of large corporations had become the nucleus of industrial innovation (Schumpeter, 1934, 1994). This shift reflected the growth of heavy industry and the advent of mass consumer culture in the United States and Europe, where large private or state-owned enterprises became the principal agents of innovation. Schumpeter's work challenged the assumption that economic growth is purely a function of capital accumulation, instead highlighting the organizational capacities that enable innovation. In the decades following Schumpeter, scholars have refined and expanded upon his ideas, introducing theoretical frameworks that underscore the complex, systemic nature of innovation. Perspectives such as innovation systems theory, the triple helix model, and evolutionary economics have each emphasized the importance of fostering networks and interactions among public and private institutions to create environments conducive to innovation (Leydesdorff, 2000; Lundvall, 2010). These diverse perspectives on innovation converge on two foundational assumptions: first, that innovation drives economic growth – without innovation economic growth is simply not possible – thereby contributing to widespread prosperity; and second, that innovation extends the limits to growth imposed by resource scarcity. In all these works, economic growth is never questioned; it is just a common-sense assumption underpinning any research on technical innovation and science, technology innovation policy (Pansera and Fressoli, 2021).

Schumpeter's work was extremely influential in shaping the technoptimism that characterises the post-World War II era. More importantly, it shaped the reaction of a part of the academic community and the political elites vis-à-vis the emergence of the environmental and social problems caused by economic growth in the 1970s. By the 1970s, in fact, environmental movements had begun to articulate concerns about the ecological risks associated with unchecked economic growth. One of the earliest and most controversial critiques of growth-oriented ideology emerged in the seminal report 'Limits to Growth', which applied systems thinking and a rudimentary assessment of Earth's biophysical limits to argue that perpetual economic growth is fundamentally unfeasible (Meadows and Randers, 2006). This report faced considerable opposition from mainstream economists of the time, who often substantiated their arguments on Schumpeter's ideas.

The influential American economist Robert Solow commented: 'The world can, in effect, get along without natural resources, so exhaustion is just an event, not a catastrophe. Nordhaus's notion of a "back-stop technology"[2] is just a dramatic way of putting this case; at some finite cost, production can be freed of dependence on exhaustible resources altogether' (Solow, 1974). More recently, Robert Solow, in an interview, contended that 'technology has to be the main part of the solution' and argued that affluent nations bear a moral obligation to enable economic development globally while respecting environmental constraints (Solow, 2002).

Let's pause for a moment and consider what Solow is actually telling us: his position hinges on the promise of *dematerialization* – the idea that technological innovation can decouple economic growth from energy and resource use, allowing production to continue indefinitely without depending on natural resources. In Solow's view, resource exhaustion is always a solvable challenge because human ingenuity and technological progress, provided the right economic incentives, can infinitely replace the material basis of life. As Bonaiuti (2023) ironically notes, neoclassical economics might lead us to believe that we can increase pizza production simply by adding more ovens and chefs – while disregarding something as essential as the dough.

Solow's ideas never stopped to be popular in mainstream academics, and they are still extremely influential in contemporary policy makers. Another economist, William Nordhaus, who like Solow was awarded the Sveriges Riksbank Prize in Economic Sciences, often erroneously called the Nobel prize for economics,[3] sustains that climate change might not be so tragic as long as we create enough wealth to pay for its damages. His analyses suggest that the economic costs of stringent climate mitigation efforts may exceed the benefits derived from avoiding the impacts of climate change (Keen, 2021).

Similar, though more articulated, arguments were used by a group of innovation scholars of the University of Sussex, who in 1973 published the book *Models of Doom* (Cole and Freeman, 1973). At the time *Models of Doom* was published, the Sussex group represented the culmination of Schumpeter's ideas revival. The Sussex team, led by the Science Policy Research Unit (SPRU), examined the methods and assumptions behind the computer-based models used in *The Limits to Growth* and found them problematic. They believed that Meadows and her MIT colleagues oversimplified the world's complex systems and presented their findings with an unwarranted sense of precision and certainty. The Sussex team argued that the World3 model – used in *The Limits to Growth* – relied on overly simplistic relationships and questionable assumptions about population growth, resource depletion, and pollution. They accused the report of ignoring important economic and technological factors, such as human innovation and adaptability, which they believed could mitigate the resource crises predicted in the report. Rather than accepting Meadows's conclusions about impending ecological collapse, the group framed the findings as 'doom-laden' and alarmist, suggesting that the models were more speculative than scientific. They emphasized that forecasting the future was inherently uncertain and that the authors of report had made bold predictions without sufficient evidence to justify them. *Models of Doom* served as a challenge to the growing influence of system dynamics models and their ability to predict global outcomes. The Sussex team pushed for more nuanced approaches to studying the future that considered economic flexibility, innovation, and complexity.

An alternative critique of *The Limits to Growth* came from the Bariloche group, which developed a model that assessed how a reorganized society could foster innovation differently to achieve both social and environmental well-being (Smith and Ely, 2025). Unlike SPRU, which focused on redistributing technological capabilities for industrialization, the Bariloche model questioned the very framework of development itself, advocating for approaches tailored to regional diversity. It proposed that productive systems should prioritize basic human needs, with development decisions guided by public participation rather than top-down economic models. Instead of being driven by the imperative to catch up with industrialized nations, technological innovation would be shaped by the specific needs of society. The model embraced a culture of egalitarian redistribution, combining social and environmental optimism, and promoted socialized ownership of the means of production. Economic growth, according to this vision, would serve the fundamental purpose of meeting and maintaining basic needs but would not be an end in itself; rather, it would remain subordinate to the broader values of a flourishing cultural life.

Both SPRU and Bariloche's critiques of *The Limits to Growth* framed the problem of economic growth as one of composition rather than sheer expansion. They argued that growth should be reimagined through a transformation of technological systems under new social and political conditions. In other words, economic growth is not a problem as long as it is directed to solve social problems. In their intentions, this would require a certain degree of direct social control over technological development. These perspectives contributed to the Vienna Declaration, a UN-backed initiative that called for a new international order based on open science and equal conditions among nations. It emphasized the right to use technology for social needs and fostered discussions on how to democratize scientific institutions, ensuring both democratic control over science and the redistribution of knowledge and technological capabilities between the Global North and South. However, these critical perspectives were gradually sidelined by the neoliberal counter-revolution, which shifted the focus from systemic transformation towards the more market-friendly concepts of sustainable development and, later, green growth. While both sustainable development and green growth frameworks incorporated environmental concerns, they largely retained a market-driven approach that accommodated existing economic structures rather than challenging them. As a result, alternative models emphasizing equity, redistribution, and democratic governance over technological and scientific progress were effectively marginalized in global policy discussions. Even more recently, despite the increasing evidence of the impossibility to decouple growth from CO_2 emissions and resource depletion (Hickel and Kallis, 2019; Parrique et al, 2019), eminent innovation scholars related to SPRU, like Carlota Perez and Mariana Mazzucato, are envisioning a bright future in which green technologies will fix the broken climate, restore economic growth, create high quality jobs, and provide a good life for everybody (Mazzucato and Perez, 2023).

The reactions to the Meadows *models of doom* all converged on preaching the potential of human ingenuity. Many preferred to believe in human beings' capacity for problem solving instead of accepting the inconvenient truth of living in a finite planet. Thus, technological change – and subsequently, innovation – became central to sustaining the vision of indefinite growth. The culmination of this reaction was the birth of the notion of Sustainable Development in the Brundtland Report (Brundtland et al, 1987). 'What is needed now', says the report, 'is a new era of economic growth – growth that is forceful and at the same time socially and environmentally sustainable'. This growth, of course, will need to be produced by technical innovations shaped and promoted by the forces of the free market. This was reinforced when the World Business Council for Sustainable Development was launched at the UN Conference on Environment and Development in Rio in 1992,[4] a milestone that marked the emergence of the idea of green growth.

Innovate or die

In today's world, innovation is celebrated as the ultimate solution to virtually all societal challenges. It's not just a buzzword; it's the cornerstone of modern governance and capitalism. Vinsel and Russell (2020) discuss how 'innovation speak' has become one of the most pervasive rhetorical devices of our time. We all need to be innovative. Governments, international organizations, and businesses alike have woven innovation into their DNA, presenting it as the driving force behind progress. As the OECD stated in 2015, 'Well-timed and targeted innovation boosts productivity, increases economic growth, and helps solve societal problems'. This belief has become so ingrained that questioning it feels almost taboo. Over the centuries, innovation has gone from being a word associated with corruption to a powerful positive force to solve problems or create new possibilities, and finally a pervasive ideology that shapes how we think about progress and development. According to Benoît Godin, innovation isn't just a flash of brilliance or a singular event. It's a total process, a holistic system that involves everyone. But there's a catch: this system is deeply oriented towards the market. The primary goal is not just to improve lives but to deliver something profitable. Even research, often viewed as a pure pursuit of knowledge for knowledge's sake, is increasingly aligned with commercial objectives. It's not about asking, 'What does the world need?' but rather, 'What will the market pay for?' Governments and global organizations have embraced this market-driven view of innovation. For instance, in 2007, OECD ministers made a bold move by mandating the creation of an innovation strategy. To them, innovation wasn't just a useful tool; it was an essential condition – a sine qua non – for achieving economic growth and boosting productivity. The underlying message was clear: innovation held the key to unlocking national prosperity. This narrative has since shaped development agendas worldwide, influencing policies in both the Global North and South (Pansera and Owen, 2018a; Jimenez et al, 2025).

In 2015 the OECD updated its approach with a strategy titled 'The Innovation Imperative'. This new vision acknowledged that innovation needed to do more than just drive economic growth; it also had to address social and environmental challenges. Governments were encouraged to build innovation ecosystems that supported inclusivity and sustainability. Innovation, it was argued, could not only make economies grow faster but also make them fairer and greener. This dual focus marked a shift in priorities. From the 1980s onward, economic growth remained central, but it became clear that growth alone wasn't enough to respond to rising societal demands for greater environmental and social improvements. If innovation was going to be the answer to these new global challenges, it needed to tackle broader concerns, like environmental degradation, social inequality, and ethical questions surrounding technology. In this context, innovation came to be seen not merely as a tool for delivering economic prosperity but as a potential solution to humanity's most pressing problems. Yet, despite these lofty ambitions, some critics argue that innovation has become hollow – more of a slogan than a genuine force for change. Godin (2020) refers to this as 'X-Innovation'. According to him, innovation today is often banal, detached from meaningful progress. It's not enough to innovate; innovation needs to be tied to something bigger – something inclusive, green, eco-friendly, or responsible. It needs a bigger mission. Without these qualifiers, innovation risks becoming an empty promise, failing to address the complexities of the modern world.

This narrow focus on market-driven innovation also profoundly shapes the governance and structure of capitalist institutions. The mantra 'innovate or die' has become a guiding principle, permeating organizational strategies across industries. Creativity and technological innovation are seen as essential to staying competitive, and courses on strategic innovation management are now staples in business education. In both public and private sectors, managing innovation effectively is considered a critical capability. It's no surprise, then, that national and regional governments compete to create programs that enhance innovation capacity. The European Union's Horizon 2020 programme, for instance, allocates billions of euros to foster innovation among its member states. Supranational entities like the OECD further reinforce this focus through guidelines and assessment tools that measure the 'innovative organization'. These tools evaluate creativity, performance, and outcomes, setting benchmarks that organizations are expected to meet. The result is a world where not just businesses but also non-profits and public institutions are pressured to prioritize innovation above all else. Even in sectors traditionally focused on social impact or public good, the language of innovation has taken over, transforming how these organizations operate (Pansera and Owen, 2018a).

Innovation for a 'better' growth or innovation for a better world?

Despite all this investment and attention to innovation, or in fact precisely because of it, we must ask ourselves: is this innovation-first approach delivering on its promises? While it's true that innovation has led to remarkable advancements – think medical breakthroughs, renewable energy technologies, and digital tools – it has also contributed to significant challenges. The OECD Oslo Manual – the guiding document for measuring and assessing the innovation capability of countries and regions, adopts Schumpeter's approach to innovation, focusing primarily on the introduction of something new while overlooking the destructive aspects inherent in the innovation process. Schumpeter's concept of creative destruction highlights that innovation not only generates novelty but also disrupts and displaces existing systems, practices, and structures. However, the Oslo Manual limits its scope to documenting the positive, productive dimensions of innovation, neglecting the often-overlooked negative consequences, such as obsolescence, social disruption, or ecological harm. This selective framing risks presenting innovation as an inherently progressive force, obscuring the complex and sometimes detrimental impacts of transformative change.

Today we have conclusive evidence that shows that many positive trends in the last two centuries, such as increasing life expectancy; wider access to energy, food and water; and the expansion of infrastructures, are almost perfectly mirrored by trends in ecosystems collapse, CO_2 emissions, ocean acidification, biodiversity loss, tropical forest disappearance, and other problems (Richardson et al, 2023). Many of these trends can be explained by technological change and innovation (for example, new technologies applied to food production have increased productivity and reduced food prices at the expense of greater pollution, higher dependence on fossil fuels, the rise of monocultures, industrial farming, and other ecologically destructive methods). Moreover, technological progress often brings unintended consequences, from job displacement due to automation to the environmental impact of mass production and consumption. The relentless pursuit of innovation can sometimes distract from deeper systemic issues. For instance, while tech start-ups race to develop the next big app, communities facing poverty, inequality, or climate crises may find that these innovations do little to address their immediate needs. This disconnect highlights the limitations of an approach that prioritizes marketability over meaningful impact. In the end, the question isn't whether innovation is good or bad – it's about who wins and who loses, what interests it serves and by which mechanisms of power. If innovation continues to be driven primarily by free market demands to fuel the fairy tale of an endless economic growth, it becomes a tool for perpetuating inequality and environmental degradation.

The dazzling promise of innovation often blinds us to its darker side – a relentless force that has reshaped the delicate balance between humanity and nature. Behind the shiny façade of progress lies a deeper reality: unchecked innovation mania has driven destructive dynamics that harm not only the environment but also knowledge systems and entire communities. The creative destruction that Schumpeter identified as the driving force of innovation was far from being merely a technical or economic phenomenon: it was, first and foremost, a social and moral one.

The constant replacement of processes and consumption goods with new ones didn't limit itself to transforming the economic sphere; it profoundly shaped social relations and our connection with the ecosystems that sustain life. This process can't be fully understood if we neglect the colonial expansion of European countries that was fundamental in supporting the emergence of Western capitalism.[5] As Sandra Harding (2011) has shown, colonialism strongly relied on technology to rationalize, command and control the colonized and their territories. Our obsession with innovation appears to reproduce this feat by constantly renovating and expanding its technical capabilities to conquer, dispossess, and exploit. Nowadays innovation processes are often articulated along complex global supply and value chains (Genovese et al, 2017). Coltan is extracted in the North Kivu mines of the Congo and shipped to Taiwan, where nanoscale semiconductors are manufactured using innovative circuits designed in California. Every year, dozens of new, higher-performance mobile phones are designed around the world and assembled in China. Most of them have an average lifespan of 2.5 years and many end up in informal or illegal dump sites in the global south (Prabhu and Majhi, 2023). This system is a direct continuation of the colonial order established at the beginning of the industrial revolution, which overlaps with the emergence of capitalism. Territories are conquered, resources are extracted, goods are shipped overseas. This has historically required a constant stream of new technologies to measure, extract, process, package, transport, and consume.

Ecocide, epistemicide, and genocide

In the last two centuries, technology has dramatically evolved, old imperial powers have declined, new ones have emerged or are rising, but the mechanisms through which technical change has negatively impacted on humans and non-humans are surprisingly similar. In the previous sections, showed that innovation is the primary driving force behind economic growth. As growth has become a kind of modern religion, it is easy to see why innovation itself has become unquestionable. However, we have also argued that the positive trends and outcomes driven by continuous innovation are often accompanied by destructive patterns. This suggests that the issue is not merely how we use innovation but the broader context in which it operates – its underlying purposes and motivations. If this is true, we cannot simply choose to use innovation for good or bad. Rather, we are fundamentally constrained by the boundaries imposed by the capitalist socio-political system, which shapes and limits technological development. This becomes evident in the fact that even innovations that appear to bring only progress often conceal hidden consequences – whether in the present, through exploitation and destruction in the Global South, or in the future, through unforeseen negative outcomes. In our opinion, these constrains have their origin in the historical process of European colonialism. As in the colonial times, in fact, today global innovation value chains still rely on three interconnected dimensions of destruction that are still functioning with an old imperialistic logic: *ecocide, epistemicide, and genocide.*

One of the most obvious and devastating outcomes of our obsession with innovation is *ecocide*: the destruction of the natural world. Forests are razed to clear land for industrial projects, rivers and oceans are polluted in the name of development, and fragile ecosystems are pushed to collapse under the weight of human ambition. This is not just environmental damage – it's the systematic dismantling of the life-support systems on which we all depend. As the Western colonisers indiscriminately hunted American buffalos to deprive native population of an essential source of livelihood, today corporations ravage the world to extract minerals and rare earths to manufacture the new electric car or the last iPhone. These extractive processes often leave behind poisoned landscapes and shattered ecosystems. Meanwhile, technologies touted as solutions to environmental crises – like geoengineering or 'green' energy projects – often create new problems while addressing old ones.[6] For instance, the mining required for electric vehicle batteries devastates entire ecosystems, contaminates water sources, and displaces local wildlife. These outcomes underscore a troubling truth: innovation, when narrowly focused on profit and marketability, often exacerbates the very crises it claims to solve.

The second dimension of innovation's destructive impact is *epistemicide*: the erasure of knowledge systems. Throughout history, the rise of colonialism and industrialization has been accompanied by the systematic dismissal and destruction of local, vernacular, and indigenous knowledge. These rich traditions, developed over centuries, represent profound ways of understanding and coexisting with nature. Yet they are often cast aside as 'outdated' or irrelevant in favour of Western, market-oriented approaches. Take, for example, the agricultural practices of many indigenous communities, which emphasize harmony with natural cycles and biodiversity. These practices have supported sustainable food systems for generations. However, global industrial agriculture, driven by innovation in fertilizers, pesticides, and genetically modified crops, has marginalized these methods. The result is a loss of knowledge that could help address modern challenges like climate change, soil degradation, and food insecurity. Epistemicide is more than just the erasure of knowledge – it is the erosion of humanity's ability to imagine diverse, adaptive solutions to global crises.

The third, final and perhaps most devastating dynamic is *genocide*: the destruction or displacement of communities in the name of progress. Innovation has often served as a tool for exploitation and oppression, from the colonial era to the present day. Technological advances have justified land grabs, forced labour, and cultural annihilation, all under the banner of development. Today, this legacy continues in subtler but equally damaging ways. Massive infrastructure projects, mining operations, and deforestation routinely displace indigenous peoples, stripping them of their lands, livelihoods, and cultural heritage. For example, the construction of hydroelectric dams often floods sacred sites and forces entire communities to relocate, severing their connection to their ancestral lands. Similarly, the extraction of resources like cobalt and lithium, essential for modern electronics, subjects workers – many from impoverished or marginalized groups – to inhumane conditions. These dynamics are also intimately intertwined with the military complex. Chris Miller (2022) documented how most of the advances in semiconductor industries were originally financed to boost the firepower of the US army. He shows how modern digital technologies are at the centre of geopolitical fights to control territories and resources. Weapons, surveillance systems, and AI algorithms represent a spectacular field for new development and businesses, especially if they can be effectively tested on the field of the multiple wars that simultaneously occur while we are writing.

The three dynamics are still today very visible in several contexts. Probably the most emblematic one is Palestine. In the occupied territories freshwater wells are filled daily with concrete, and ancient olives trees are set on fire or eradicated by the Israeli army or violent illegal settlers.[7] In the meantime, a constant hammering propaganda denies the very existence of Palestinian identity and culture.[8] Finally, ethnic cleansing and physical extermination characterize the Israeli colonial process of dispossession. The second Trump administration's plan to ethnically cleanse Gaza is a clear example of these dynamics.[9] It's particularly ironic how this campaign has been carried out by Israel, considered one of the most dynamic, entrepreneurial, and innovative states. In his book *The Palestine Laboratory*, Anthony Loewenstein (2023) shows how the Israel innovative 'start-up' state model is essentially based on technological spillovers coming from decades of experiments on controlling, guarding, and killing Palestinian civilians. Probably the most disturbing product of this system is the Lavender system, an AI tool developed by Israel's Unit 8200, part of its military intelligence. Lavender is said to analyse large amounts of data to identify individuals in Gaza as targets by assigning them risk scores, ranging from 1 to 100. It uses machine learning to detect behavioural patterns or connections that link individuals to Hamas or militant activity. Investigations allege that this AI-driven process may have led to large-scale civilian casualties, as human oversight during target verification is minimal – often as little as 20 seconds per target before approval for strikes. The system often considers residential buildings with even minor militant links as legitimate targets, even if bombing them results in significant civilian harm (Iraqi, 2024). More recent investigations suggest that the Israeli army is building an AI language model using millions of intercepted conversations between Palestinians, which could accelerate the process of incrimination and arrest (Abraham, 2025).

These three dimensions – ecocide, epistemicide, and genocide – are not isolated phenomena. They are deeply interconnected, driven by the same systems of power and profit that underpin innovation mania. Together, they expose the illusion of progress that dominates modern thinking about innovation and growth. Far from being universally beneficial, this relentless focus on technological advancement often deepens inequalities, erases diverse ways of knowing, and wreaks havoc on the planet. Breaking free from this cycle requires reimagining the purpose and direction of innovation. Instead of being a tool for unchecked growth, innovation can and should prioritize equity, sustainability, and respect for all forms of life. Imagine a world where technological advances are guided not by profit but by a commitment to preserving ecosystems, honouring diverse knowledge systems, and protecting the dignity of all communities. This shift requires a fundamental rebalancing of values – one that embraces the complexity of humanity as a dynamic interplay of competition and cooperation, creativity, and care. It means questioning the dominant narrative that innovation is always good and recognizing that some forms of progress come at too high a cost. It also requires amplifying the voices of those who have long been marginalized – indigenous communities, local farmers, and activists who advocate for a more balanced relationship with the planet. Their insights, often dismissed in the rush to innovate, hold the key to building a more inclusive and sustainable future. The relentless pursuit of innovation has brought humanity to a crossroads. By acknowledging the interconnected harms of ecocide, epistemicide, and genocide, we can begin to dismantle the systems that fuel these destructive dynamics. Only then can we chart a path forward – one that prioritizes not just growth but the well-being of all living beings and the planet we share. The promise of innovation must be redefined to serve a vision of progress that uplifts, sustains, and connects rather than divides and destroys.

One of the problems with this 'innovation mania' is the set of implicit assumptions embedded within it. As scholars like Strand et al (2018) point out, these assumptions include beliefs that technological innovation inherently yields more societal benefits than harms, that it leads to increased employment and higher wages, and that greater efficiency in technical systems reduces resource consumption and enhances sustainability. These assumptions, while optimistic, often go unchallenged, even when evidence suggests otherwise. Underlying these assumptions are three deeply ingrained beliefs. The first is *technological determinism* the idea that technological development is inevitable and unstoppable. This perspective frames technological progress as a force of nature, something we can't and shouldn't resist. The second belief is *productivism* – the notion that innovation drives economic growth, prosperity, and job creation, and that these outcomes are always beneficial. The third is the *illusion of control* – the faith in human ingenuity to steer the products of technology and control its effects. Together, these beliefs create a framework that precludes alternative visions of growth and development. They foreclose democratic debates about what kind of future we actually want, limiting the scope of action for governments, communities, and individuals. In the next chapter, we analyse the construction of these two myths. We start by situating the discourse of innovation within the wider totalizing ideology of growth, then we dismantle the logics of technical determinism and productivism drawing on the degrowth and post growth literatures and the contributions from science and technology studies (STS).

TWO

What's Wrong With Innovation and Why it Matters for a Post Growth Society

The critique of economic growth has a long history, but few thinkers have articulated it as powerfully as the French philosopher André Gorz. At the end of the 1970s, Gorz was challenging the idea that the pursuit of economic growth is a necessary precondition to improving human welfare. Being an active trade unionist, Gorz was very well aware of the intimate relation between capitalism, the growth imperative, and the push for technological innovations that were both destroying nature and alienating workers in the factories of the epoch. He was equally critical of how socialist economies, such as the USSR, became fixated on growth, viewing mass industrialization and the adoption of increasingly productive technologies as a means to outcompete their capitalist counterparts. For Gorz, any serious emancipatory project for the working class had to begin by challenging the pursuit of endless economic growth, regardless of whether this growth was pursued in the name of capitalism or socialism.

The fading promises of growth

After almost five decades, Gorz's ideas are more relevant than ever. Historically, the pursuit of economic growth rested on a set of promises: higher living standards, better public services, more fulfilling jobs, and greater economic stability. Yet growth was never framed as merely an economic goal. It was also tied to a broader vision of societal progress – freedom, democracy, peace, equality, and environmental protection. Growth was not just beneficial; it was seen as the necessary and sufficient condition for these outcomes. Accordingly, more growth meant more freedom. More growth meant greater democracy. More growth meant rising equality and a cleaner environment. And, of course, more growth meant better jobs, better public services, and greater economic stability. These were the promises. Yet they have largely gone unfulfilled. Rather than delivering on its guarantees, growth has deepened inequality, accelerated environmental degradation, and intensified social alienation.

Extensive critiques of these failures exist elsewhere (for example, Kallis et al, 2025; Jackson, 2009), so we won't rehearse them here. Instead, we highlight a more fundamental issue: growth became a utopian project across the political spectrum, increasingly detached from reality – a hegemonic ideology in which expanding production and consumption was assumed to be a universal remedy for all societal and environmental ills, as Herman Daly and other critics have pointed out. The more these promises failed to materialize, the more the pursuit of economic growth became an act of faith – a blind commitment to an ideology that has repeatedly fallen short. And the more this happens, the more relevant Gorz's prescient ideas become.

Beyond the growth paradigm: what role for science, technology, and innovation?

Many have proposed alternatives like a steady state economy (Daly, 2008), an a-growth economy (van den Bergh, 2011), a doughnut economy (Raworth, 2017), or a degrowth paradigm (Kallis, 2018) in which a planned and democratic downscaling of the economy can be achieved without compromising collective welfare and ecological well-being. There's already a wealth of post growth policy proposals covering a range of areas, from work to consumption (Fitzpatrick et al, 2022). Additionally, there is a lively debate around post growth strategy – specifically, how to bring about the necessary changes and who should lead this transition (Barlow et al, 2022). This debate spans a spectrum of approaches, from top-down initiatives to more bottom-up, grassroots efforts.

However, within post growth debates, only a few studies have focused on the importance of rethinking the role of science, technology, and innovation. As we discussed in the previous chapter, the past four decades have witnessed a revival of Schumpeter's ideas. Accordingly, the notion of innovation has become intimately attached to the idea of economic growth. Technological innovation, fuelled by applied science, improves productivity and efficiency, which, in turn, boost economic growth. Innovation is often framed as the lifeblood of competitive advantage, essential for organizational survival and success. Accordingly, stopping the flow of innovation is seen as catastrophic – almost a heresy – for any organization in a market economy (Bessant et al, 2005). The logic is straightforward: innovation drives efficiency, slashes cost, creates standout products, and boosts quality – all of which help organizations outshine competitors, win customers, and grow their market share. In this view, which has become the received wisdom, innovation equals growth: more sales, bigger markets, and long-term success. This narrative is so pervasive that it presents organizations with what seems like a binary choice: *innovate or die*. The pressure to innovate is framed as non-negotiable, a prerequisite for survival in an ever-changing, hyper-competitive world. Because innovation is often described in terms of efficiency and technical progress, its politics are hidden. It's indeed widely treated as a process that is best described by following a technical rationality, seemingly independent of values or social context. To put it simply, innovation is often framed as just about solving technical problems – making things faster, cheaper, or better – without considering the bigger picture: *Who benefits? Who decides what problems to solve? And what values are driving these decisions?*

We believe that this narrative of innovation underpins three deeper assumptions. First, that technology development is inevitable – *technological determinism* – and second, that the more innovations the better – *productivism*. Third, no matter how complex and pervasive our technologies become, we will always be in control – *the illusion of control*. It is not difficult to see that this perspective leaves no space for alternative socio-technological imaginaries about growth and development and closes down any possibility of a democratic and participative debate about what futures we as a society, community, or group of individuals desire (Pfotenhauer et al, 2019).

Technological determinism

Technological determinism is based on the idea that technological change (often fuelled by science) is inevitable and always desirable. STS studies show that this assumption is very problematic. STS scholars have shown that technical change, far from being a neutral and autonomous process, reflects the values, ideologies, and worldviews of the society in which it evolves. To be more precise, often these are the values and worldviews of the dominant elites (Winner, 1980; Jasanoff and Kim, 2009). That means that technology evolution doesn't not follow a steady evolutionary progress forward but is more likely to proceed by a succession of leaps forward and periods of stagnation (Callon, 1991; Bijker, 1995). For example, the space race between the United States and the Soviet Union saw rapid advancements during the Cold War, with milestones like the first satellite, the Sputnik in 1957, the first human in space, Yuri Gagarin in 1961, and the moon landing the Apollo 11 in 1969. However, after the collapse of the USSR in 1991, space exploration slowed significantly due to reduced funding and political shifts. It remained relatively stagnant until the twenty-first century, when private companies like SpaceX reignited progress with reusable rockets and ambitious plans for Mars exploration. In this view, a certain path of technological change is enabled by specific socio-economic conditions, convergences of interests and historical circumstances that can or can't occur. What's more is that multiple paths of technological change are possible and often coexist at the same time, although over the time one might become hegemonic. Once a certain technological path becomes dominant, it goes through a process of *naturalization* that creates the illusion that this is the only possible way of doing things, an inevitable progress of human ingenuity. Hence, what looks like an inevitable evolution is often the result of convergent interests, asymmetric power relationships, and, in many cases, systems of domination and violence.

We often assume that the predominance of private cars is a natural condition of modernity, a logical and inevitable outcome of technological progress. In particular, within the United States, owning a car has become deeply ingrained as a cultural symbol of individual freedom, independence, self-sufficiency, and progress. However, the widespread adoption of private automobiles was far from organic or inevitable. It was the result of deliberate planning and active promotion by a coalition of powerful interests, including automobile manufacturers, fossil fuel industries, urban planners, and policy makers. To enable the rise of the automobile, cities had to be fundamentally reshaped. Infrastructure like highways, extensive road networks, and parking facilities were prioritized and rapidly constructed, often at the expense of existing urban layouts and public spaces. This transformation occurred during an era when public transportation systems were already highly advanced and effective. For instance, England boasted an extensive railway network connecting towns and cities, and tram systems were the backbone of transportation in most major European capitals. Yet, public transit systems were gradually dismantled or neglected to accommodate the car-centric model. What we see today – the dominance of private cars worldwide – is not a natural or inevitable result of progress but a carefully engineered outcome, driven by economic and political interests.

This phenomenon is not unique to the rise of automobility; similar dynamics occur across many other sectors. Take, for instance, the energy industry. Today, most of us accept without question that a handful of large, centralized energy companies monopolize electricity production and distribution. It feels 'natural' and more efficient to rely on vast, privately owned power plants that deliver energy seamlessly to homes and businesses. However, this centralized energy model is just one possible pathway among many. In reality, alternative ways of producing and distributing energy exist – and they are gaining momentum. Across Europe, for example, energy communities are flourishing. These are decentralized, community-owned, democratically managed organizations focused on renewable energy production. Such models empower local communities to produce, manage, and consume their energy sustainably. One notable example is Som Energia,[1] a Spanish renewable energy cooperative in which most of the electricity is generated and supplied directly by cooperative members. By prioritizing local, clean energy solutions, cooperatives like Som Energia demonstrate that alternative systems can be both viable and beneficial. The broader lesson here is clear: multiple technological pathways are almost always available. Yet, the dominance of one technology or system over others – whether it be private cars or centralized energy production – is often not an inevitable outcome but a result of deliberate political, economic, and social choices. Recognizing this reality encourages us to question assumptions about 'progress' and explore alternative solutions that align with values like sustainability, equity, and community empowerment.

From those seeking to challenge technological determinism, a crucial question arises: what is the connection between the new and the already existing? For Schumpeter, in the most deterministic way, innovation was inherently disruptive – the new must displace the existing, violently so if necessary, in what he famously described as 'creative destruction'. If technological change is an evolutionary process, and the dynamics of market competition demand constant change, then societies must avoid becoming too attached to existing knowledges, infrastructures, technologies, or ways of doing. After all, technological progress follows a linear path, where some technological innovations displace others purely based on their superior performance and the rational advantages derived from their adoption. But the reality of how innovation processes unravel in the world is not so simple.

In 2014, during fieldwork in the Indian state of Gujarat, one of us encountered a Microsoft-led campaign aimed at addressing illiteracy through high-tech applications. The initiative, while well intentioned, overlooked a crucial reality: local teachers had already developed innovative and highly effective methods for teaching children complex Gujarati characters – methods that were often simpler, more affordable, and better adapted to the local context. In a personal interview, Professor Anil Gupta, founder of the Honey Bee Network – an organization dedicated to studying and supporting grassroots innovations – raised a thought-provoking question: why were Indian media, academics, and policy makers so eager to celebrate high-profile literacy programs from global tech giants like Microsoft and IBM? These projects, often grounded in digital and high-tech solutions, were given disproportionate attention. Meanwhile, the efforts of rural teachers who had devised over a hundred educational innovations to accelerate literacy in Gujarat alone went virtually unnoticed. These grassroots solutions, carefully documented by the Honey Bee Network, thrived without any governmental support or corporate funding (Pansera and Owen, 2018b). This example illustrates a broader pattern: alternative solutions to dominant technological pathways always exist. Yet, they are frequently ignored, marginalized, or dismissed in favour of high-tech, Western-centric approaches that are perceived as superior or inevitable. This dynamic is not unique to education; it reflects a deeper historical process in which technology has been wielded as a tool of colonial domination in the Global South. Technologies introduced by colonial powers often silenced, erased, or displaced pre-existing knowledge systems, cultural practices, and indigenous ways of living. The discourse of technological inevitability – the idea that Western technology represents the pinnacle of progress and is, therefore, unavoidable – has often served to justify and impose transformations in the productive and social systems of colonies and former colonies. These changes, while framed as 'modernization', have historically favoured the economic and political interests of colonial powers, reinforcing systems of dependence and exploitation (Escobar, 2004). Recognizing this legacy allows us to critically assess whose interests are served by dominant technological choices and to elevate the value of alternative, context-specific innovations. Local solutions, like those created by rural educators in Gujarat, not only demonstrate ingenuity but also challenge the notion that technological progress must always follow a single, top-down, or high-tech trajectory. Instead, they reveal the potential for inclusive, decentralized, and culturally grounded pathways to development – pathways that respect and build upon the knowledge of local communities.

Andrew Feenberg suggests that the concept of technological determinism mirrors the assumptions of Whig history:[2] it projects the inevitability of an outcome backward onto its origins, as if the final form of a technological object were predestined from the very beginning (Feenberg, 1992). This narrative erases the contingency, complexity, and social choices that shape technological development, reinforcing the illusion of a single, inevitable path to progress. The technical logic of a finished artefact cannot be divorced from the historical, cultural, and social conditions that produced it. By neglecting these dynamics, determinism naturalizes technological outcomes, obscuring the role of human agency, power, and competing alternatives in shaping the evolution of technology.

This deterministic lens has far-reaching implications for the way we perceive technology's relationship to society. As Langdon Winner (1993) observed, social constructivist analyses – despite revealing the social origins of technological artefacts – have often hesitated to confront the broader social issues and power structures embedded in these processes. This is where post growth and degrowth scholars and activists must intervene. Beyond critiquing specific technological systems, they should expose the ideological underpinnings of technological 'progress' and offer pathways towards more democratic, sustainable, and equitable alternatives.

Feenberg's critical theory of technology provides a valuable framework for this task. He argues that technological design is not neutral but rather reflects the social rationality of its time. For instance, the structures of industrial machines, such as those used in chain production, embody the logic of rationalization and hierarchy that defined modern capitalist systems (Feenberg, 2001). By mirroring and reinforcing prevailing social relations, these technological forms become instruments of hegemony – tools that solidify the dominance of specific economic and political interests while presenting themselves as natural and inevitable. This perceived neutrality of technology – the functional rationality of machines and systems – further entrenches its role as a legitimizing force. When technological choices are hidden or framed as apolitical, the deterministic narrative prevails, justifying existing social orders under the guise of 'progress' and 'efficiency'. In reality, these choices are far from inevitable. As Feenberg emphasizes, alternative technological pathways are always possible. The suppression of these alternatives – whether through neglect, marginalization, or active erasure – ensures that dominant systems remain unchallenged, serving the interests of the few while limiting the agency of the many. To counter this, we must recognize technology as a site of struggle – a space where competing social values, interests, and visions of the future intersect. By reclaiming the power to make explicit choices about technological alternatives, we challenge the deterministic image of technology and disrupt its role as an unquestionable driver of social order. This requires exposing not only the hidden choices behind dominant technologies but also elevating grassroots innovations, alternative practices, and democratic forms of technological development. Only then can we move beyond the illusion of inevitability and begin to imagine – and enact – technological futures that align with principles of justice, sustainability, and collective well-being.

Productivism

The second problematic assumption, productivism, is based on the idea that innovations lead to economic prosperity; the creation of new jobs; new, more efficient products and services; and that the 'new' is a good in itself. Robust empirical evidence exists that more innovative economies show higher growth rates (Fagerberg and Verspagen, 2009). What is less clear are the distributive effects of innovation and their impacts on inequality. Evidence suggests that economic growth boosted by innovation can actually exacerbate existing inequality levels. This is because innovation tends to reinforce dominant market actors, limit the access of certain resources and social goods to specific societal sectors or quickly disrupt traditional (in some case more sustainable) ways of doing things (for example, Walmart vs small local shops, agrobusiness vs traditional agroecological practices) (Cozzens and Kaplinsky, 2009; Cozzens and Thakur, 2014).

When it comes to the debate on employment, advocates of innovation have consistently argued that while new technologies may render certain jobs obsolete in the short term, their long-term impact on employment is always positive. This optimism is rooted in the belief that innovation drives increased productivity, which, in turn, creates new opportunities, economic growth, and ultimately, better jobs. In reality the relation between innovation and employment remains complex and highly contested (Pianta, 2006; Bogliacino and Pianta, 2010). What is evident, however, is that innovation increases labour productivity, but it is not sufficient to provide well-being or escape poverty. Especially when productivity gains are appropriated by few powerful. According to the ILO Global Wage Report in 2012, the labour productivity index from the 1970s increased much more than the real wage index, which indicates that wealth created is not being equally distributed between labour and capital (Piketty, 2014). As André Gorz (1980) has convincingly demonstrated, the elimination of social exclusion, poverty, and unemployment can never be accomplished by increasing production alone, which is the implicit goal of the mainstream way of framing innovation. A clear example of André Gorz's argument can be seen in the case of automation and technological advancements in industrial production, particularly within the automobile industry. According to Gorz, the widespread adoption of industrial robots and automated assembly lines revolutionized car manufacturing in the 1980s. While these technological innovations dramatically increased production efficiency, enabling factories to produce more vehicles at lower costs, they also led to significant job losses. Automation reduced the need for human labour, particularly displacing low- and medium-skilled workers who could no longer compete with machines. Rather than creating new opportunities, innovation excluded many from employment altogether, leaving workers to face long-term unemployment or precarious, lower-paying jobs. Even as productivity and profits soared for manufacturers, the benefits of this progress were not equally distributed. Executives, shareholders, and those in highly specialized roles enjoyed substantial rewards, while those left out of the system experienced heightened poverty and exclusion. This unequal distribution of gains illustrates the core of Gorz's critique: increasing production alone cannot solve unemployment or social inequality. The focus on perpetual growth and efficiency as the ultimate goals of innovation often intensifies inequality, as those who are already marginalized are further excluded. The case of automation shows that the problem lies not in technological progress itself but in the way it is framed and pursued within mainstream economic systems. By prioritizing production and growth over social well-being, structural issues, such as unequal access to resources and protections, remain unaddressed. Gorz argues that overcoming poverty, unemployment, and exclusion requires a fundamental shift: innovation must be reimagined not as a tool to maximize production but as a means to enhance equality, autonomy, and collective well-being. Without such a reorientation, technological advancements will continue to deepen, rather than resolve, social divides.

The illusion of control

In addition to technological determinism and productivism, a third assumption underpinning mainstream innovation perspectives is the belief that technological change, while disruptive in the short term, will eventually grant those who embrace it greater mastery, predictability, and control over the social and natural world. In the book the *Left Hand of Darkness*, the science fiction writer Ursula K. Le Guin says: 'The only thing that makes life possible is permanent, intolerable uncertainty; not knowing what comes next'. This sentence condenses all our present adrenaline addiction caused by a continuous gambling on new, untested, uncertain, often unneeded technologies. We tend to overemphasize the potential benefits but often totally neglect the potential consequences – most of the time because they are simply unpredictable. In fact, while innovation is often celebrated for its ability to solve pressing problems, it frequently operates in an ungoverned or poorly regulated manner, which can create new and often unforeseen social and environmental challenges. Macnaghten and Owen (2011) highlight this paradox by emphasizing that technological solutions, when pursued without sufficient oversight or reflection on their broader implications, often have unintended consequences. These consequences can exacerbate existing inequalities, harm ecosystems, or undermine social well-being, ultimately requiring further interventions to address the very problems innovation creates. For instance, the rapid development and deployment of plastic materials in the mid-twentieth century provided a groundbreaking solution to several industrial and consumer needs. Plastics were cheap, durable, and versatile, revolutionizing fields as diverse as packaging, medicine, and construction. Initially seen as an innovation that addressed material scarcity and improved convenience, plastic production was widely adopted with little consideration of its long-term environmental and social implications. Decades later, the widespread use of plastics has resulted in severe environmental degradation, with microplastics contaminating oceans, wildlife, and even human bodies.[3] A solution to one set of problems – affordable materials and efficient production – created a cascade of new problems, including pollution, biodiversity loss, and human health risks.

A similar dynamic can be observed in digital technologies and the rise of the so-called gig economy. Digital platforms like ride-hailing or food delivery services promised flexibility, convenience, and economic opportunities. They solved logistical and labour challenges by connecting workers and consumers through innovative apps. However, in the absence of governance and regulatory foresight, these platforms have also fostered new social issues, such as precarious working conditions, wage insecurity, and the erosion of labour rights. Workers in the gig economy often lack access to basic protections, such as health insurance, a stable income, or job security, further deepening existing inequalities while benefiting a few dominant tech companies. On a larger scale, ungoverned innovation in energy systems exemplifies how technological 'solutions' can generate environmental and social dilemmas. Fossil fuel technologies, for example, were celebrated as innovations that enabled industrialization and economic development, solving issues of energy scarcity and facilitating unprecedented levels of productivity. Yet, the widespread adoption of fossil fuels has contributed to climate change, air pollution, and environmental destruction, leading to health crises, ecological breakdown, and the displacement of vulnerable communities. Innovation in this context solved immediate energy needs but at the cost of long-term planetary and human well-being. Other examples can be found in the way we uncritically deployed nuclear plants, GMO crops, and all sort of chemical compounds and additives. The list is endless.

Macnaghten and Owen's critique points to the need for responsible innovation – an approach that anticipates and reflects on the broader consequences of technological advancements (Owen et al, 2021). Innovation cannot be treated as an inherently neutral or purely beneficial force. Its trajectory must be shaped by ethical considerations, inclusive governance, and democratic deliberation to ensure that it addresses societal challenges without creating new ones. Left ungoverned, innovation risks perpetuating cycles of harm, where short-term solutions exacerbate long-term social and environmental problems. Instead, by integrating sustainability, equity, and accountability into the innovation process, we can work towards technological developments that genuinely improve collective well-being without leaving behind a trail of unintended consequences.

Towards a repoliticization of technological innovation

The problem with proponents of technological determinism, productivism, and the illusion of control lies in their failure to recognize that innovation is not an autonomous or inevitable process; it is inherently socially, culturally, and politically constructed. As Stirling (2015, p 19) aptly states, 'innovation is fundamentally about the politics of contending hopes'. In this sense, innovation is neither singular nor inevitable but rather plural and conditional. What constitutes a 'good' innovation is not universally agreed upon because multiple, often contrasting pathways can hold equal validity. The appropriateness of any innovation depends on changing perspectives and specific social, political, and environmental circumstances (Bussu, 2014). Technological determinism erases this plurality by reducing innovation to a singular and inevitable trajectory, ignoring its diverse possible outcomes. Productivism, on the other hand, neglects the political questions at the heart of innovation: Who decides what is good or bad? Who benefits, and who loses? By what mechanisms of power are these choices made? For example, when productivity increases, do we use it to reduce working hours, raise wages, or increase dividends for shareholders? Such critical questions are rarely considered in mainstream innovation discourse.

Building on this, an essential insight comes from thinkers such as Jacques Ellul and earlier critics like Ernst Jünger. These scholars emphasized that technological development, when left unchecked, can become uneconomic – that is, its damages can outweigh its benefits. In works like The Technological Society (Ellul, 1964), this pessimistic perspective argued that humans risk becoming enslaved by technology and a purely technological mode of thought. Jünger (1949) shared a similar sentiment, seeing technological progress as a force that, if unchallenged, strips away human autonomy. However, this pessimism was forcefully countered in the 1970s by alternative views that called for reorienting technological change to serve social justice, freedom, and ecological balance rather than perpetuating economic growth. Thinkers such as Murray Bookchin, André Gorz, and Fritz Schumacher offered pathways for a more humane and sustainable technological development. Bookchin's (2004) notion of liberatory technology argued for tools that foster autonomy and social equity. Gorz (1980), in turn, developed an ecology of tools, focusing on technology that supports human flourishing while respecting ecological limits. Schumacher (1973) introduced the concept of appropriate technology, which emphasizes small-scale, localized, and sustainable tools that meet human needs without causing environmental harm.

At the same time, Ivan Illich's (1973) *Tools for Conviviality* offered a powerful critique of uncontrolled technological expansion. Illich argued that unchecked technological change risks creating tools that grow beyond human control, leading to social and ecological unsustainability. He warned of the overgrowth of technologies that disrupt ecosystems, concentrate power, and undermine user autonomy. As a counterbalance, Illich proposed the idea of convivial technology,[4] tools designed to enhance ecosystems, empower individuals with autonomy and control, disrupt inequitable power structures, and remain durable, robust, and adaptable. It is important to note that Illich, Gorz, Schumacher, and, above all, Bookchin never embraced primitivism or an anti-technology stance. While each had distinct perspectives, they all advocated for rebalancing or limiting large technological systems. More importantly, they emphasized the need to develop institutions that enable direct social control over technology.

In conclusion, the direction of technological innovation is not predetermined; it is a matter of political and societal choice. Its consequences are frequently unpredictable and may evade control, leading to unintended and often harmful effects. Innovation must be critically examined and shaped to serve goals beyond economic growth – namely, social justice, ecological sustainability, and democratic forms of participation. Only by embracing the inherent plurality of technological possibilities and asking difficult questions about power, benefits, and consequences can we move towards technologies that align with the needs of post growth societies. Such a perspective challenges the dominant productivist framework and opens pathways towards a more just and convivial technological future. What are the implications for degrowth and post growth practitioners and activists? A substantial number of degrowth thinkers have presented radical positions about technology that have been tagged as anti-technology or even modern forms of Luddism. A movement of working-class artisans in nineteenth-century Britain protested against the introduction of new machinery, particularly in the textile industry, fearing job losses and declining living standards. If innovation is an essential driver of economic growth, which has become socially and environmentally unsustainable, are we condemned to reject creativity, inventiveness, and human ingenuity? Our answer is certainly no. We think that the modern idea of innovation narrowly framed within the parameters of free market capitalism is a miserable and despicable view of human creativity. In the next chapters we provide an alternative view of innovation based on four main topics: *innovation as caring for people and for things*, *innovation as alternative forms of organizing*, *reflexions on scale and complexity*, and, finally, a discussion about what would mean a *radical democratic way of governing technology*. Each chapter will couple an introductory conceptual critique with empirical examples of alternatives.

THREE

Caring and Maintaining

It's a sunny day just outside Naples, and we're off on a little family adventure – kids, grandpas, and all – heading to see one of the area's most fascinating Roman treasures: the Piscina Mirabilis. Hidden away in Baia, this ancient underground wonder feels like something out of a storybook. You step down into its cool, shadowy depths and suddenly find yourself surrounded by towering stone pillars that stretch up to a vaulted ceiling, like a cathedral carved beneath the earth. It's hard to believe that this was once just a giant water tank, built in the first century AD to supply the Roman fleet stationed nearby at Museum. The Piscina Mirabilis is enormous, measuring 70 meters long, 25 meters wide, and 15 meters high – big enough to hold around 12,000 cubic meters of fresh water. Standing there, it's easy to feel small, dwarfed by the sheer scale of it. Yet what makes this place truly special isn't just its size or the engineering brilliance of its grid of 48 massive pillars: it's the Roman approach to maintenance. As the guide explained, the reservoir is a monument to care and upkeep. The Romans designed it to last – not to be replaced, rebuilt, or 'updated' year after year. It was built to be maintained, and that's why it still stands today, centuries later, silently waiting, still functional in its own way.

Walking through this ancient cistern, with sunlight sneaking through cracks above and the kids' voices echoing off the stone, you can't help but marvel at the Romans' ingenuity. They understood something that seems almost forgotten today, which is the value of building things to endure, to be cared for over time. The Piscina Mirabilis is a testament not only to Roman engineering but to the power of patience, maintenance, and thoughtful design. It's as if the past is whispering to us, reminding us that sometimes the most remarkable creations are the ones built to last. We shouldn't forget though that such a marvel was not only the fruit of human ingenuity but also of slavery, oppression, and domination. Marvellous things made to last for centuries thanks to the suffering of hundreds of men and women. The grandeur of the Piscina Mirabilis also serves as a reminder of the social inequalities underpinning such achievements. The labour of enslaved and oppressed individuals fuelled its construction, demonstrating that even acts of extraordinary ingenuity often bear the imprint of exploitation. This juxtaposition of ingenuity and inequity serves as a foundation for rethinking innovation itself, moving away from narratives of destruction and replacement towards practices of care, maintenance, and repair.

The myth of seamless innovation and the realities of a world falling apart

When everything works, maintenance and repair fade into the background. Infrastructure is taken for granted – until it fails. A bridge safely carries commuters for decades, until one day, it collapses. A power grid delivers electricity seamlessly – until a storm knocks it out, revealing just how fragile the system truly is. As Susan Leigh Star (1999) famously put it, this is a 'call to study boring things': the often-overlooked labour that sustains our daily lives. A working subway system, a well-maintained highway, or a functioning water supply rarely capture public attention, but the moment they break down, their significance becomes undeniable. We celebrate invention – the next big thing – while maintenance remains undervalued. Comedian John Oliver captures this bias well: 'Building is fun, destroying is fun, but a Lego maintenance and repair set would be the most boring fucking toy in the world.' The sentiment resonates because we are conditioned to think of progress as creation, not preservation.

Yet this mindset is not universal. While Western culture often prioritizes constant innovation, in many parts of the world, repair, maintenance, and repurposing are not just options but necessities driven by economic constraints and cultural practices. In Cuba, for example, ingenious mechanics keep 1950s American cars running through creative adaptations and locally fabricated parts. In India, the concept of jugaad encapsulates a tradition of frugal innovation, where households fix broken appliances with improvised solutions. Likewise, in numerous African cities, vibrant informal repair economies enable technicians to extend the life of smartphones and laptops that Western consumers have already discarded. These examples remind us that when repair and maintenance are valued, technology can have not only long but also multiple lives (Radjou et al, 2012).

This contrast highlights a structural issue in modern capitalism. We are accustomed to measuring progress in terms of new inventions, economic growth, and increased productivity – but these metrics obscure the labour that sustains our world. As Lee Vinsel and Andrew Russell (2020) argue in *The Innovation Delusion*, societies have become obsessed with the mythology of innovation while failing to recognize that most of what makes life possible comes from maintenance, repair, and care. The vast majority of technological life is not about breakthroughs – it is about upkeep. The world is not a seamless web of self-sustaining systems. Instead, it is a fragile network of aging infrastructures, crumbling roads, and legacy technologies – held together by an underappreciated force: maintenance labour.

What if all repair and maintenance simply stopped? In *The World Without Us*, Alan Weisman (2008) asks his readers to picture a world where humans suddenly disappear overnight. Without the constant, behind-the-scenes maintenance work that keeps our modern technological systems and infrastructures running, everything would start falling apart surprisingly fast. Subway tunnels might flood within days; roads, bridges, and buildings would begin to crumble within years; and before long, nature would reclaim entire cities. Weisman's thought experiment exposes a surprising paradox – our modern technological and engineering systems may seem permanent, but they're actually quite fragile, relying on ongoing repair, patching, and updating to fend off nature's inevitable decay. And this fragility isn't just about physical structures – it extends to software, industrial supply chains, and global networks, all of which need constant maintenance to function.

This paradox underpins Steven Jackson's (2014) notion of 'broken world thinking'. Jackson challenges the myth of seamless technology by showing that most infrastructures spend much of their time in disrepair, adaptation, or partial breakdown. Rather than acknowledging this inherent fragility, economies and governments pour resources into flashy new projects, ignoring the slow, unglamorous labour of upkeep. The outcome is a world that prizes novelty over stability, disposability over durability.

The social and ecological costs of neglect

When we ignore the routine labour required to sustain our bridges, roads, and power grids, we set the stage for catastrophic failures that have far-reaching consequences. Take the 2018 Genoa bridge collapse as an example. As Russel and Vinsel (2020) note in *The Innovation Delusion*, the Morandi Bridge failed not due to a lack of technological innovation but because of years of neglected maintenance. The disaster killed dozens, highlighting the real-world stakes of failing to invest in upkeep. Similar patterns play out daily in underfunded infrastructure worldwide, where governments prioritize flashy new projects over maintaining existing ones. The cost of this neglect is borne disproportionately by lower-income communities, who are most affected when public infrastructure deteriorates.

The same pattern of neglect extends beyond public infrastructure. If the bridges, roads, and power grids that sustain daily life are left to deteriorate, consumer goods fare no better. In fact, some industries actively prevent repair and maintenance to drive sales and boost economic growth. Planned obsolescence – the intentional design of products with artificially limited lifespans – has become a dominant business strategy, forcing consumers into unnecessary replacements (Guiltinan, 2009). When essential products like household appliances, smartphones, and cars are designed to be unrepairable, wealthier consumers may be able to absorb these costs. However, for lower-income households, replacing a broken washing machine or laptop instead of fixing it can mean financial strain. Disadvantaged communities are thus disproportionately impacted by repair barriers, as they are compelled to participate in an economy that forces them to repurchase what could otherwise be repaired (Perzanowski, 2022). Ecologically, this model generates staggering levels of waste. In 2022 alone, the world produced over 50 million metric tons of electronic waste (Forti, 2018), much of it from products discarded not because they were beyond repair, but because they were designed to be unfixable. The waste crisis is compounded by the fact that much of this discarded material is shipped to lower-income nations, creating toxic 'waste colonies' in places like Agbogbloshie, Ghana, and Guiyu, China (Lepawsky, 2018). These sites expose workers – often children – to hazardous chemicals as they extract valuable metals from discarded electronics, illustrating how waste externalities are unequally distributed. Therefore, neglecting repair and maintenance is not merely about isolated breakdowns. Such neglect not only drives waste and environmental decay but also deepens social inequities by shifting the burdens of failure onto those who can least afford them. At its core, this is an economic and political choice, not an inevitability. Recognizing the value of repair means challenging this system – shifting from a culture of disposability to one that values sustainability, fairness, and long-term thinking.

Innovation as care: learning to love our monsters through repair and maintenance

Caring can be understood as the full range of actions we take to sustain, preserve, and repair our world so that life can flourish. This world encompasses our bodies, our individual identities, and our environment – all intricately woven into a complex, life-supporting network (Fisher and Tronto, 2003). Genuine care requires us to start from the perspective of those who need attention. It means meeting others ethically by adopting their viewpoint and understanding the world as they do. Caring compels us to extend our commitment beyond our bodies and immediate surroundings – so, if we truly nurture our interconnected world, shouldn't our technological creations receive the same tender care?

Yet, despite this ideal, our current system tells a different story. The materialistic bond between people and technology promoted by growth-driven innovation is far from affectionate. As we shown in previous chapters, the prevailing discourse on innovation is rooted in Joseph Schumpeter's paradigm of creative destruction: the old must be ruthlessly torn down to make way for the new. This view celebrates rapid technological advancement, relentless cycles of consumption, and the inevitability of obsolescence. It ignores the ecological and social costs of such relentless progress. It valorizes novelty at the expense of sustainability, perpetuating a throwaway culture. It casts our creations as disposable commodities, fuelling an endless chase for novelty while neglecting any long-term commitment. In today's system, gadgets vanish before they have a chance to mature, and infrastructures are abandoned when upkeep becomes too costly. What if, in a post growth world, innovation meant rethinking our approach – learning to love, nurture, and care for our technologies, infrastructures, and material artefacts rather than discarding them at the first sign of trouble?

Bruno Latour (2011), in his essay 'Love Your Monsters: Why We Must Care for Our Technologies as We Do Our Children', challenges us to bridge this disconnect. He argues that our technological creations are not mere tools but products of collective ingenuity that continue to shape our social and ecological landscapes. For Latour, loving our 'monsters' requires three key orientations:

- Accountability: Because technology is a collective creation, it is not enough to cast blame when things go wrong. We must actively oversee its effects, recognizing that our inventions continue to shape social and ecological realities long after their launch. Accountability, in this sense, is also a process of learning from both failures and successes to guide better design and upkeep.
- Care, not disavowal: In a culture of disposability, malfunctioning technologies are often discarded without hesitation – severing the vital moral and practical ties that bind us to our creations. Instead, choosing to repair and maintain these systems becomes an act of genuine care. Each repair is not merely a technical fix but a reflective process that teaches us about durability, resilience, and design principles hidden beneath the allure of novelty.
- Critique of 'Back to Nature': Latour draws on Mary Shelley's *Frankenstein* to illustrate that the true danger is not in creating technological 'monsters' but in abandoning them. Shelley's narrative reminds us that failure lies in walking away from our creations once they emerge. By committing to guide and maintain them – and learning from their behaviours and limitations – we can steer future innovations towards more sustainable, resilient paths.

Feminist philosopher Puig de la Bellacasa, in her work in *Matters of Care: Speculative Ethics in More Than Human Worlds*

(2017), offers another crucial perspective. She redefines care as a deeply relational, ethical, and affective practice that goes beyond simple human-to-human interaction. For her, care is not merely an act of benevolence but the very foundation of maintenance and sustainability. Her notion of 'speculative ethics' challenges us to view every repair not just as a technical necessity but as an opportunity to learn, adapt, and forge deeper connections with the world around us. In doing so, every act of repair contributes to our collective wisdom and resilience.

Loving our technologies means more than chasing the latest gadget – it is about embedding moral commitments in the devices and infrastructures that shape our everyday lives. Imagine a world where broken smartphones are not immediately discarded, where aging bridges and crumbling water systems are restored with a deliberate focus on understanding their vulnerabilities, and where each repair informs better design and more resilient practices. In this vision, repair and maintenance become dynamic processes of learning that honour the collective wisdom woven into our creations. In other words, care provides the ethical and practical orientation needed to respond to this reality. Repair, then, becomes a form of care – not just a technical activity but a commitment to sustaining and valuing the material world and the people that depend on it.

The politics of care as a democratic project

We place care at the centre of post growth innovation, yet feminist thinkers remind us that care is never apolitical – it is deeply intertwined with power dynamics and contested social struggles. The same happens with repair. Here, it's worth quoting Graziano and Trogal (2019, p 227), who, from a feminist perspective, argue that 'repair shares with broader practices of care and social reproduction a recalcitrance to be reduced to a regime of practice that is inherently or intrinsically "good"'. While care is a vital value, it has often been idealized and undervalued, with the burden of care falling on those with the least power. Historically, women – and increasingly migrants – have shouldered care labour, forming 'global care chains' where essential work is extracted from marginalized groups to sustain wealthier societies (Todaro and Arriagada, 2020). This uneven distribution not only perpetuates inequality but also devalues care work itself.

André Gorz (1989) argued that capitalism forces us into a division of labour between productive and reproductive (or care) work, where productive labour is privileged, while care work is systematically outsourced. To work fulltime, for example, many workers must delegate their care responsibilities – a division of labour that is only viable when care work is systematically unpaid or grossly underpaid relative to productive labour. This dynamic is evident in the fields of technology and innovation, too. While professions within the creative class of technologists and engineers are celebrated for designing new innovations and shaping our digital future, the work of repair and maintenance – which actually sustains our technological and material world – remains among the most undercompensated forms of labour (Llorente-González and Vence, 2020). In short, even as society glorifies novel designs and breakthrough technologies, the indispensable labour that keeps these systems functioning is largely ignored, deepening inequality and rendering our infrastructures increasingly vulnerable to failure. Ultimately, reimagining care in our material world is as much a democratic and political project as it is a technical one. By recognizing that our infrastructures – and the labour that sustains them – are deeply intertwined with social inequality and environmental vulnerability, we expose the hidden costs of a culture obsessed with novelty. This understanding demands that we reclaim repair and maintenance as vital, democratized acts of care.

The repair movement embodies this shift towards care. It challenges the proprietary restrictions and planned obsolescence that force our technologies into disposability, advocating instead for policies that empower individuals and communities to keep their devices, machines, and systems functioning sustainably. With this perspective in mind, we now turn to the right-to-repair (R2R) movement – a transformative force poised to reshape our relationship with technology and to foster a culture where repair is celebrated as an act of genuine, democratic care.

The right-to-repair movement

In recent years, original equipment manufacturers (OEMs) have increasingly restricted consumers' and independent repair shops' ability to fix everyday products. These barriers take many forms, including limiting access to spare parts, requiring proprietary tools and diagnostic software, designing products in ways that make disassembly difficult, enforcing warranty policies that discourage third-party repairs, and using legal mechanisms, such as copyright claims on repair manuals or digital rights management, to block unauthorized fixes (Perzanowski, 2022). These restrictions make the practice of autonomous and independent repair costly, technically difficult, inconvenient, and, in some cases, legally challenging for consumers and independent repairers. In another work we argue that OEMs impose these restrictions to consolidate control and establish monopolies over essential repair services for two main reasons (Lloveras et al, 2024). The first, and most direct, is to deter repair and encourage product replacement – a strategy commonly associated with planned obsolescence. However, in other cases, the goal is not to prevent repair and maintenance altogether but to turn these services into a controlled revenue stream. By restricting access to essential repair tools, software, and parts, manufacturers transform repair from an independent practice into a service that consumers must purchase on the company's terms. This model allows OEMs to profit not only from selling products but also from maintaining exclusive rights over their upkeep, locking consumers into costly service agreements and preventing competition from third-party repair providers.

Against this backdrop, the R2R movement has emerged as a loose coalition of actors with diverse stakes in repair access, from independent repair shops and environmentalists to farmers, military personnel, and technology enthusiasts. Pro-repair businesses, such as Fairphone, Framework, and Backmarket, alongside grassroots repair initiatives and consumer advocacy groups, all contribute to a growing push for repair-friendly policies. Their demands include not only more repairable product designs but also greater access to essential repair resources – spare parts, specialized tools, repair manuals, and diagnostic software – along with the removal of software barriers that hinder third-party and self-repair.

This tension between the R2R movement and corporate opposition is not just a matter of technical feasibility – it reflects broader political and economic struggles over control, autonomy, and resource access. While manufacturers claim that repair restrictions ensure consumer safety, prevent intellectual property infringement, and protect brand integrity, critics argue that these justifications serve to entrench corporate monopolies and extend product control beyond the point of sale (Perzanowski, 2022). At stake are fundamental questions about technological citizenship and democratic rights: who has the authority to intervene in technological systems? Who benefits from the repair economy? And how do current regulatory frameworks either reinforce or challenge corporate dominance over maintenance and repair? Most crucially, how can different communities reclaim and exercise greater democratic control over the essential repair and maintenance systems on which their livelihoods, infrastructures, and collective well-being depend?

While unified in demanding more accessible repair practices, the R2R movement is composed of different ideological and strategic perspectives. These differences do not automatically converge under the R2R banner. For example, a conservative-voting farmer in the United States who supports R2R legislation for agricultural equipment may share little in common with environmental activists in the EU pushing for repair as a sustainability measure. Similarly, tech-savvy hackers advocating for open-source hardware may not see eye to eye with consumer protection groups focused on corporate accountability.

In this regard, it is important to recognize the discursive activity required to build shared meanings around R2R. The movement is not a natural alliance but a coalition that must be actively constructed. Different actors must engage in framing repair in ways that resonate across ideological and social boundaries. This process involves finding common ground while maintaining distinct motivations and objectives. Four primary frames structure the movement: *consumer rights, environmentalism, grassroots innovation,* and *communitarian repair* (Lloveras et al, 2024).

- The *consumer rights* frame emphasizes ownership and freedom of choice, arguing that individuals should have the right to fix what they own without being forced into expensive manufacturer-controlled repair services. This perspective is particularly appealing in legal and economic debates, as it aligns with broader concerns about market fairness, anti-monopoly policies, and consumer welfare.
- The *environmental frame* positions repair as a means of reducing waste and extending product lifespans to mitigate ecological harm. This argument has gained traction in regulatory discussions, particularly in the EU, where repairability is increasingly linked to climate policy. However, tensions arise when corporations attempt to co-opt environmental narratives, promoting limited manufacturer-controlled repair programs while continuing to design products with built-in obsolescence.
- The *grassroots innovation frame*, often associated with the maker movement, open-source advocates, and repair

hackers, sees repair as a creative and empowering act. This perspective challenges proprietary restrictions, arguing that repair is not just about fixing but about modifying and improving technologies. This frame comes into conflict with corporate efforts to impose software locks, digital rights management, and legal barriers that restrict independent repair and innovation.
- Finally, the *communitarian repair frame* focuses on repair as a collective activity that strengthens local resilience. Community repair initiatives, such as Repair Cafés and Fixit Clinics, promote skill-sharing and mutual aid, challenging the notion that repair should be a for-profit service. This frame highlights the social and economic inequalities that emerge when repair access is restricted, positioning repair as a tool for empowerment and inclusion.

These frames do not always align perfectly, but their coexistence allows the movement to appeal to diverse stakeholders. The challenge for R2R advocates is to navigate these differences without fragmenting the coalition. Rather than seeking a singular, unified agenda, the movement benefits from maintaining a pluralistic strategy that allows different actors to align where their interests overlap while continuing to advance their distinct priorities. This discursive flexibility is essential for challenging corporate control over repair and shaping policy reforms that support repair accessibility across different sectors and contexts.

While these four frames offer distinct set of meanings about what the R2R should be, they are interconnected. Consumer rights and environmentalism have been particularly influential in shaping legislation, while grassroots and communitarian repair provide practical alternatives to corporate monopolies. Some of these demands are starting to make inroads into policy making, especially in the United States and the EU, where R2R regulations have already been implemented, and more are currently under discussion.

After extensive advocacy and campaigning, the EU adopted the Right to Repair Directive (Directive (EU) 2024/1799) on 13 June 2024, aiming to promote sustainable consumption by facilitating the repair and reuse of consumer goods. The directive mandates that manufacturers offer repair services for products beyond the standard two-year legal guarantee, extending up to ten years depending on the product category. It also requires producers to provide spare parts and tools to independent repairers at reasonable prices, although specific guidelines on what constitutes 'reasonable' are yet to be defined. To enhance transparency, the directive introduces a European Repair Information Form, allowing consumers to obtain standardized repair quotes, and establishes an online platform to connect consumers with repair services. However, the directive's scope is limited to certain products already subject to EU repairability requirements, such as washing machines, dishwashers, refrigerators, and electronic displays. Critics argue that this narrow scope and potential loopholes may hinder the creation of a truly fair repair market in Europe.[1]

As of early 2025, the R2R movement has achieved significant milestones across the United States. Notably, all 50 state legislatures have introduced Right to Repair bills over the past eight years, reflecting widespread support for consumers' ability to repair their own devices. Currently, 24 states have active legislation, with approximately 50 bills filed or carried over in 2025 alone. Since 2020, seven states have enacted nine versions of such laws, underscoring the growing momentum of the movement. Major corporations, including Google, Microsoft, and Apple, have shifted from opposing to supporting this legislation in various states, indicating a significant industry change. Advocates emphasize that the universal introduction of these bills highlights a nationwide demand for repair autonomy and consumer rights. However, challenges remain, particularly concerning the scope and enforcement of these laws, as some manufacturers continue to implement practices that may limit independent repairs.[2]

The right to repair as an ongoing democratic struggle over repair systems: implications for post growth innovation

At first glance, innovation is celebrated as the creative spark – those 'bright and shiny' moments of technological origination – while repair and maintenance are seen as mundane, secondary processes that merely fix what goes wrong. However, as Steven Jackson (2014) argues, this separation is misleading. The impact of innovation is not realized at the moment of invention but through its extension, adaptation, and survival in the real world. Repair is not an afterthought to innovation; it is what completes it. It ensures durability, mitigates breakdowns, and makes technology workable over time. This is why R2R is not merely a legal or technical issue but a deeply political one (Graziano and Trogal, 2019). It represents a democratic struggle over who controls repair, who decides what can be fixed, and who determines the lifespan of the objects we depend on. It exposes the monopolization of maintenance systems, the enclosure of technical knowledge, and the broader consequences of allowing corporate interests to dictate when something is 'beyond repair' (Lloveras et al, 2024).

The essence of the R2R resides primarily in its potential to radically democratize repair systems, creating agonistic spaces for contesting hegemony. Such conceptualization confronts OEMs and policy makers with new ethical questions regarding what should be repaired (and what shouldn't), who should have the right to repair it, and under what institutional conditions can this right be democratically exercised. These questions matter to post growth innovation for two reasons. First, because they push current ethico-political thinking beyond a focus on economic incentives, technical efficiencies, and behavioural outputs, to draw attention to a plethora of societal ramifications stemming from the unchallenged acceptance of hegemonic co-option of repair (for example, the monopolistic power and structure of repair and maintenance systems, the limits of intellectual property in the context of repair, the impact of repair restrictions on consumers' well-being and welfare, the erosion of community resilience and alienation of users, and so on). The fight for repair is, at its heart, a rejection of the idea that technologies are disposable. It asks us to recognize that even mass-produced objects can be objects of care.

Up to this point, we have treated repair and care as synonymous. But should they always be? An absent question in the R2R movement is whether all technologies should be subject to repair – or whether, in some cases, we might need a right *not* to repair. In this sense, we might return to Bruno Latour (2011) and ask: do we really need to learn to love all the monstrous creatures that modern, growth-driven innovation systems have created? Private jets, SUVs, and military equipment, for instance, embody extractive, ecologically destructive, or violent systems that should not be sustained indefinitely. If repair is a form of care, then maintaining certain technologies raises an ethical contradiction: should we extend the life of machines that reinforce social inequality, accelerate climate collapse, or perpetuate warfare?

This shifts the repair debate beyond mere consumer rights and into the terrain of democratic technological governance. Just as R2R challenges corporate monopolies over maintenance, a post growth framework must also consider the politics of obsolescence. Some technologies should not be endlessly repaired and kept in circulation but instead actively decommissioned, dismantled, or phased out. Care, in this sense, is not just about preservation but also about letting go – about recognizing when maintaining a system does more harm than good. This dual perspective – the right to repair and the right to not repair – reorients innovation away from an indiscriminate push for technological longevity and towards a deeper political and ethical engagement with what should be sustained and what should be abandoned. It challenges us to think critically about which futures we maintain and which we allow to end.

In reflecting on the insights of this chapter, several transformative messages emerge. First, true innovation is reimagined as an act of care rather than mere creation. The Piscina Mirabilis stands as a powerful testament to this idea: it was built not only to serve a practical function in its time but to be maintained through generations. This challenges us to rethink our modern fixation on novelty and disruption by recognizing that lasting ingenuity is rooted in ongoing care. A second realization is that neglecting the labour of maintenance carries profound consequences. Russell and Vinsel (2020) rightly observe that 'the most unappreciated and undervalued forms of technological labour are also the most ordinary: those who repair and maintain technologies that already exist, that were "innovated" long ago'. And this, of course has consequences: When the continuous effort required to sustain infrastructures and technologies is undervalued, the hidden costs emerge as societal fragilities, ranging from environmental decay to the disproportionate burden on marginalized communities. This perspective compels us to appreciate maintenance as the backbone of functional systems rather than an afterthought. The third key message underscores that repair and maintenance are inherently political. The struggle to secure repair rights is not merely about fixing objects but about reclaiming democratic control over technological systems that have been increasingly monopolized by corporate interests. This contestation transforms technology into a 'parliament of things', where competing visions of society and civilization are negotiated through practices of care and repair. Fourth, the chapter calls for a redefinition of progress in a post growth context. Instead of measuring success by a constant churn of new products, we are invited to value longevity, adaptability, and ethical stewardship. This shift in perspective moves away from the relentless pursuit of economic growth and towards a more sustainable vision where technological evolution is balanced with preservation and renewal. Finally, the insights demand a critical ethical reflection on what should be preserved. Not all technologies warrant indefinite repair; some systems, due to their detrimental impacts, might be better off decommissioned. This dual perspective – the right to repair and the right not to repair – challenges us to discern which legacies to nurture and which to let fade, ultimately aligning our technological futures with principles of social and ecological justice.

Post growth innovation then, must be understood not as a series of isolated breakthroughs but as an ongoing commitment to ethical stewardship and collective care. It calls for integrating maintenance and repair into the innovation lifecycle – ensuring that every new technology is designed with longevity, adaptability, and equity in mind. Rather than celebrating novelty for its own sake, post growth innovation now demands that we critically assess the full life cycle of our technologies: from their creation and deployment to the often-overlooked labour of upkeep and, when necessary, the deliberate decision to retire systems that do more harm than good. In this reframed perspective, progress is measured not solely by economic or technological gains but by our ability to nurture systems that support social justice, environmental sustainability, and democratic participation.

FOUR

Organizations and Institutions for Post Growth

Innovation doesn't happen in a vacuum. It happens in and through organizations. Before we proceed, it's important to clarify what we mean by 'organization'. Here we follow Martin Parker (2018, p 75), who argues that '"organization" simply refers to patterns of people and things that humans arrange in order to get things done, the outcome of the patterning of people, technology and finance. It is a big word, a generous word, and it doesn't need to be reduced to "management"'. From multinational corporations to states, to worker cooperatives and trade unions, the ways in which people organize and the organizations they create are potentially limitless, adapting to different needs, contexts, values, and geographical scales. Once established, these collective entities that we recognize as organizations not only shape how people continue to organize but also influence their actions and perceptions of the world. And in doing so, they shape our relations with innovation and technology.

This broader perspective challenges the idea that organization is inherently tied to centralized management, businesses, or, indeed, economic growth, instead revealing a vast landscape of organizing practices that structure social and economic life in diverse ways. Organizing and organization, both as a verb and a noun, are tied to innovation. The kinds of technologies, business models, and social practices that emerge are shaped by the organizations that develop and implement them. In economies built around perpetual growth, organizations — whether corporations, start-ups, or public institutions — are structured to maximize output, efficiency, and market expansion. As a result, they tend to favour innovations that drive productivity, financial returns, and consumption. However, this model is increasingly being challenged. If economic growth is neither necessary nor desirable for long-term well-being, how must organizations change in order to support innovation beyond growth?

Across different fields and communities, people are beginning to imagine new ways of innovating that don't rely on constant growth. These alternative models have sprung up in a wide range of contexts, from grassroots organizations and public institutions to private companies and cooperatives. They show that there's no one-size-fits-all answer but rather a rich diversity of responses to the challenges our growth-driven systems pose. Some of these models harken back to earlier ideas, like the appropriate technology movement, which emerged to champion tools and solutions that empower local communities rather than prioritizing industrial-scale production. Others focus on grassroots innovation, where local knowledge and resources are leveraged to create solutions tailored to specific needs. Cooperatives, with their emphasis on shared ownership and collective decision-making, also provide an example of how economic activity can be organized around principles of equity and sustainability rather than profit maximization. Meanwhile, open-source and collaborative production models highlight how innovation can flourish when knowledge and tools are shared freely. These approaches challenge the conventional wisdom that progress depends on competition and exclusivity. Instead, they show how creativity and development can thrive in environments built on collaboration, transparency, and shared goals.

What ties these different approaches together is their shared commitment to redefining the purpose of innovation. Rather than focusing on large-scale industrialization or fuelling consumer dependency, these models prioritize local empowerment, autonomy, and democratic engagement. They challenge the assumption that 'bigger' or 'faster' automatically means 'better' and instead advocate for innovation that serves people and communities directly. These examples offer glimpses of a future where innovation isn't just a tool for growth but a means to build more equitable, participatory, and sustainable systems. By looking to these alternative frameworks, we can begin to reimagine what progress might look like when it's untethered from the relentless pursuit of expansion. Instead, innovation can become a way to create resilience, foster collaboration, and meet the needs of people and the planet alike.

Post growth organizations

The appropriate technology movement, which gained prominence from the 1970s to the late 1980s, was instrumental in inspiring various grassroots innovation movements worldwide (Kaplinsky, 2011). Its advocates promoted the development of technologies tailored to the specific needs and capacities of local communities. Such technologies were designed to be affordable, easily maintained, and reliant on local resources and labour, contrasting sharply with the capital-intensive, centralized, and often imported technological solutions that characterized conventional development approaches (Darrow and Pam, 1978). Proponents of appropriate technology aimed to foster social equity and environmental responsibility by enabling communities to take control of technological processes that would benefit their well-being and resilience. This movement reacted against the widespread practice of imposing Western industrial technologies, which often failed to address the socio-economic and infrastructural realities of low-income regions, resulting in abandoned projects and unmet development goals (Carr, 1985).

Central to the appropriate technology movement were the ideas of economist Fritz Schumacher (1973), who argued for 'small is beautiful' solutions that prioritize human-scale development over large-scale industrialization. Schumacher's work, alongside the critiques of thinkers like Ivan Illich, influenced development workers disillusioned by post-World War II models of industrialization that emphasized North–South technology transfer. The movement underscored the limitations of one-size-fits-all development models and highlighted the importance of context-sensitive approaches that empower local communities to take ownership of technological solutions. Appropriate technology proponents primarily targeted small, rural communities where poverty and inequality were most pronounced, advocating for sustainable, small-scale interventions that align with local capacities (McRobie, 1981).

In the decades following the appropriate technology movement, grassroots innovation movements emerged and continued to evolve, driven by similar principles of community empowerment and sustainability. Scholars have identified key grassroots movements in developing countries, including the People's Science Movement and the Honey Bee Network in India, and the Technologies for Social Inclusion movement in Latin America (Smith et al, 2014). These initiatives emphasize participatory development and democratized knowledge production, challenging traditional innovation models that rely on centralized control and hierarchical decision-making. Grassroots innovation has also gained traction in industrialized countries, where scholars have documented community energy projects, socially sustainable food networks, and alternative burial practices (Hargreaves et al, 2013; Kirwan et al, 2013; Ornetzeder and Rohracher, 2013). These experiments reflect a shift towards local, user-led innovation, with community members taking active roles in designing and implementing solutions that address their specific needs and environmental concerns.

An important feature of grassroots innovation is its potential to serve as a catalyst for broader socio-environmental transitions. Scholars argue that grassroots initiatives provide an alternative framework for thinking about sustainable futures, opening up space for debate and experimentation outside of mainstream growth-oriented models (Seyfang and Haxeltine, 2012; Feola and Nunes, 2014). Such innovation practices prioritize autonomy, distributed knowledge, and horizontal collaboration, challenging traditional power dynamics and fostering inclusive approaches to problem-solving (Avelino et al, 2019). The DIY and makers' movements, characterized by a do-it-yourself ethos and enabled by digital technology, are examples of grassroots innovation in action. Platforms like iFixit and initiatives focused on technological disobedience (*desobediencia tecnologica*), such as the work of Ernesto Oroza in Cuba,[1] embody the R2R philosophy, pushing back against planned obsolescence and promoting sustainable, community-led alternatives to corporate-controlled production (Matchar, 2016; Oroza, 2019).

The Social Technology Network (STN) in Brazil provides another example of non-growth-oriented innovation. Established in the early 2000s during the administration of President Lula da Silva, the STN sought to integrate the resources of the Brazilian state and public enterprises with grassroots initiatives to improve access to essential resources in impoverished communities. This network facilitated the large-scale implementation of selected grassroots technologies (Fressoli and Dias, 2014). Some notable examples include the 'cisternas de placa', a simple yet effective rainwater harvesting system that provides clean water to communities in Brazil's semi-arid regions and benefited over 600,000 households; 'fogões ecológicos', energy-efficient stoves that reduce firewood consumption and indoor pollution; and biodigesters, which convert organic waste into biogas for cooking and electricity. These technologies, developed through participatory processes, empower marginalized communities by improving living conditions while preserving the environment. Unlike traditional development models, the STN rejected patents and emphasized small-scale, context-specific solutions that aligned with the principles of appropriate technology and were consistent with the broader goals of Brazil's social movements, such as solidarity economy and agroecology. The STN faced tensions between the desire to scale up impactful projects and the need to preserve small-scale, community-based approaches, underscoring the challenges inherent in balancing expansion with sustainability and local empowerment.

Social cooperatives, which originated in Italy in the 1970s, present another alternative to growth-focused innovation. Recognized legally in the 1990s, these cooperatives operate according to principles that contrast with traditional capitalist organizations, including alternative ownership structures, funding models, and decision-making processes (Pansera and Rizzi, 2020). Grounded in the Italian tradition of civil economy, social cooperatives are guided by principles of reciprocity and solidarity, aiming to fulfil communal needs rather than maximizing profit (Bruni and Zamagni, 2007). Italian Law 381, enacted in 1991, formalized the role of social cooperatives in integrating disadvantaged groups into society, supporting individuals who face barriers to employment, such as the disabled, former inmates, and immigrants (Thomas, 2004). This legislative recognition facilitated the spread of social cooperatives across Italy and other European countries, fostering a model of enterprise that prioritizes human welfare over growth. Social cooperatives have demonstrated the viability of operating alongside capitalist firms without compromising their ethical principles. For instance, they have made significant inroads in fields such as recycling, retail, and social care by replicating their cooperative model across different sectors rather than expanding individual organizations (Parker et al, 2014). By avoiding growth and focusing on replication, these cooperatives maintain their democratic, horizontal structures, which they believe would be compromised by scaling up.

Similar approaches can be found in community-based enterprises globally, which emphasize local empowerment and sustainable development over profit maximization (Peredo and Chrisman, 2006; Dentoni et al, 2018).

Finally, the open and collaborative production movement has emerged as a powerful model of non-growth-oriented innovation. Beginning with the open-source software movement in the mid-1980s, this model has expanded into various fields, including citizen science, open hardware, common based peer production, and community-based prototyping spaces, like FabLab and makerspaces (Robra et al, 2023). A contemporary example of this experimental activity is the P2P Lab, based in Ioannina, Greece, a research collective dedicated to exploring the intersection of peer-to-peer practices, open-source technologies, and sustainable development. As a key partner in the ERC-funded project Cosmolocalism,[2] the P2P Lab investigates how locally based production, supported by global knowledge-sharing networks, can foster innovation and sustainability without relying on traditional growth paradigms. Cosmolocalism emphasizes the idea of 'design global, manufacture local', where digital knowledge and open designs are shared globally, while physical production is localized, reducing the environmental impact and empowering communities (Papadimitropoulos, 2024). The P2P Lab's work bridges theoretical research and practical experimentation, focusing on how open-source collaboration and decentralized manufacturing can create resilient local economies. Through case studies, pilot projects, and collaborations with diverse stakeholders, the lab contributes to rethinking innovation as a process rooted in equity, ecological awareness, and collective creativity.

More generally, open-source initiatives challenge conventional assumptions about innovation by demonstrating that large-scale collaboration can occur without traditional hierarchical organization or intellectual property restrictions (Benkler, 2016). For instance, the open-source Linux operating system has grown into a widely used platform, rivalling proprietary software in terms of performance and reliability, thereby underscoring the potential of collaborative, non-proprietary approaches to innovation (Weber, 2005). Open-source projects, like Linux, Wikipedia, and Galaxy Zoo, illustrate the capacity of distributed knowledge production to harness diverse expertise and 'the wisdom of the crowds' (Surowiecki, 2004). These initiatives benefit from the inclusivity and openness of their licensing models, allowing individuals from various backgrounds to contribute freely. Open licences not only facilitate innovation by separating management from ownership but also protect contributors from exploitation by powerful entities, as they enable unrestricted sharing and modification of content (Weber, 2005). The open-source ethos has inspired similar initiatives in other fields, promoting a collaborative, non-growth-oriented approach to knowledge and resource sharing that empowers individuals and communities to create solutions on their own terms.

In our ERC-funded project Prospera, we also directly documented several cases of collectives who are struggling to repurpose innovation. For example, CoopCycle is a striking example of how organizations can challenge growth-centric paradigms and operate under the principles of post growth (Fortuny-Sicart et al, 2024).[3] Founded in 2017, CoopCycle is a federation of food delivery cooperatives that has reimagined the platform economy by placing worker autonomy, democratic governance, and social equity at the centre of its operations. Unlike traditional delivery platforms that prioritize profits and centralize control, CoopCycle's cooperative model allows its members – local delivery cooperatives across the globe – to co-own and co-govern the platform. This shift from shareholder-driven decision-making to collective ownership reflects the values of post growth organizations, which prioritize sustainability, fairness, and community well-being over unchecked economic expansion. At its core, CoopCycle demonstrates how innovation can be redirected to align with post growth principles. The cooperative has developed its own logistics software, designed collaboratively by workers and developers, to meet the specific needs of its members. This participatory approach not only ensures that the technology supports the collective interests of the workforce but also challenges the extractive logic of traditional platforms. By using a copyleft licence, CoopCycle prevents the commercial exploitation of its software by profit-driven entities, ensuring that the platform remains a tool for social empowerment rather than becoming a vehicle for private gain. CoopCycle's governance model is another hallmark of its post growth orientation. Each cooperative in the federation has an equal vote in decision-making, regardless of its size or financial contributions. This commitment to egalitarian governance ensures that power is distributed fairly and that the voices of smaller or less resourced cooperatives are not overshadowed. The federation also provides training and support to its members, helping them navigate the challenges of running cooperatives in competitive markets.

By pooling resources, sharing knowledge, and fostering collaboration, CoopCycle creates a resilient network that thrives on mutual aid rather than competition. Moreover, CoopCycle's focus extends beyond economic considerations to address broader social and environmental goals. By promoting local delivery services that rely on bicycles, the federation reduces the environmental footprint of its operations. Additionally, it actively supports marginalized groups, including migrants and precarious workers, by providing opportunities for dignified and equitable employment. Initiatives like the Maison des Coursiers, a support hub for delivery riders in Paris, highlight CoopCycle's commitment to care and solidarity, offering resources, advocacy, and a sense of community for workers often excluded from traditional labour protections. CoopCycle exemplifies how post growth organizations can operate in a way that balances economic viability with social and ecological responsibility. It challenges the conventional wisdom that progress and innovation must be tied to growth, showing instead that organizations can thrive by prioritizing care, cooperation, and sustainability. By building a model that rejects the extractive practices of platform capitalism, CoopCycle offers a tangible blueprint for how organizations can align with the principles of a post growth economy and create systems that are equitable, participatory, and resilient.

Most of the cases we documented are experiments (sometimes failed) of collectives and bottom-up civil society groups (Schramm et al, 2024). For example, Go-op is the UK's first cooperative train operating company,[4] founded in 2010, and is focused on creating rail services that prioritize local needs, environmental sustainability, and social inclusion. It plans to operate a rail service connecting towns like Taunton and Swindon, addressing the lack of connectivity in underserved areas of Somerset and Wiltshire. The cooperative's structure embodies its post growth ethos, operating as a multi-stakeholder cooperative with three groups of members: travellers, workers, and non-user investors. This setup aspires to ensure democratic governance while allowing essential external investments in this capital-intensive sector. Go-op's approach exemplifies post growth innovation by rethinking the role of transportation systems within local communities. Instead of focusing on growth through increased passenger volumes or expanded routes, Go-op aims to enhance regional connectivity and reduce car dependency. By tailoring their service to the specific needs of local communities, the cooperative challenges the growth-oriented logic of mainstream transport operators. However, navigating complex regulatory frameworks and a monopolized rail infrastructure has presented significant challenges.

Another case is The Big Lemon,[5] founded in Brighton in 2007, which reimagines bus services to align with social and environmental values. Initially powered by locally collected cooking oil, its buses transitioned to solar energy in 2017. Operating routes in Brighton, Bristol, and Bath, the company focuses on underserved areas and low-frequency routes often overlooked by commercial operators. Its operations emphasize sustainability, community engagement, and providing accessible, enjoyable public transport. Post growth innovation is at the heart of The Big Lemon's model. By running on renewable energy sources, the company challenges the reliance on fossil fuels that dominates traditional transport systems. Its focus on community ownership, with funding from local bonds, shareholders, and local communities, shifts power away from centralized, profit-driven models. Furthermore, The Big Lemon prioritizes social goals such as creating dignified work environments and tailoring services to meet specific community needs. These practices reflect a commitment to local empowerment and resourcefulness over relentless expansion. Even as the company has grown and expanded to new cities, it continues to balance its original mission with the operational realities of the transportation sector, demonstrating how post growth innovation can evolve within a practical framework.

Finally, Railcoop, established in 2019, is France's first railway cooperative, dedicated to reviving underused and abandoned rail lines. Its flagship project aims to restore the Lyon-Bordeaux route, discontinued by SNCF in 2014. Operating as a cooperative with over 14,000 members, Railcoop combines local community engagement with collective investment and governance, ensuring that its priorities align with social and environmental goals rather than profit maximization. By focusing on regional connectivity and reducing car dependency, Railcoop aspired to provide a tangible alternative to the high-speed rail services that dominate France's privatized system. Its cooperative model reflects the principles of inclusivity and democratic governance, challenging the centralized control of traditional rail operators. Railcoop faced liquidation due to financial issues in the spring of 2024.[6] Nevertheless, it can be considered an experiment of transport system that priorities equitable access, sustainability, and resilience over efficiency and expansion.

Post growth organizations' distinctive features

The example of organizations discussed above distinguish themselves from growth-oriented ones through several defining characteristics that shape their environments and the innovative solutions they generate. Although none of the cases exposed can be unequivocally defined as 'post growth' organizations, we can still propose a number of features that clearly distinguish them from conventional business as usual organization. Drawing on our previous work (Pansera and Fressoli, 2021), in Table 1 we suggest nine dimensions that contrast post growth organizations with growth-oriented ones.

The foundational difference lies in their core values. Growth-oriented capitalist organizations innovate within competitive

Table 1: Growth-oriented organizations vs post growth-oriented organizations

Dimension	Growth-oriented organizations	Post growth-oriented organizations
Underpinning values	Profitmaking Competition A-cultural Value-free	Social justice and equality Cooperation, autonomy, and self-sufficiency Culturally specific Overtly normative
Underpinning resources	Organizations that benefit from commodification of common resources pools (for example, water, land, natural resources, public goods) and labour.	Organizations that oppose commodification and appropriation of the commons. Valorize or reinforce community democratic control over technology.
Ownership and governance	Privately owned, management led, controlled by private board. Increasingly characterized by trans-national forms of ownership.	Diverse forms of ownership (for example, worker-owned coops, community ownerships, local ownership, family ownership, distributed ownership).

Table 1: Growth-oriented organizations vs post growth-oriented organizations (continued)

Dimension	Growth-oriented organizations	Post growth-oriented organizations
Production/ consumption patterns	Export-oriented, fragmented, geographical and social division of labour. Tendency to separate production/producers from consumption/consumers.	Oriented to local markets. Tendency to involve consumers in the decision-making process of the producers.
Surplus	Surplus is usually reinvested to increase total factor productivity. In general, there is no democratic mechanism to decide how surplus is invested.	Surplus can be either reinvested to increase factor productivity or redistributed among the participants. In any case, the decision-making process tends to be democratic.
Intellectual property	Organizations that usually (with few exceptions) favour strong intellectual property regimes.	Open-source, free-licences, distributed forms of knowledge production.
Technology design	Expert design, highly reliant on science output, planned obsolesce, constant search for novelty.	Expert plus diffused participatory design. Tendency to produce *convivial forms of technology.*
Power relationships	These organizations are usually embedded in socio-economic clusters that tend to escape democratic control. They enjoy the support of political elites and scientific institutions.	These organizations usually rely on local social network. Some explicitly challenge dominant power structure in search of social emancipation and autonomy.
Scale	Variable scale with a tendency to huge aggregations and oligopolies.	Reduced scale, tendency to reproduce the model instead of scaling up.

Source: Pansera and Fressoli, 2021

environments to gain advantages, ultimately prioritizing profit maximization. Even when these organizations adopt measures like corporate social responsibility or adapt to frameworks such as the B-Corp model (Chen and Kelly, 2015), they often remain value-neutral and operate independently of cultural or member-specific contexts (Gibson-Graham, 2006). In contrast, post growth organizations focus on innovation that is normatively driven, targeting social and ecological concerns above all else. Their solutions are culturally specific and guided by principles of social justice and equity. From the case of CoopCycle, which frames technology as a way to fight back the abusive labour conditions of delivery corporations, to the P2P Lab, which seeks to dynamize local communities in rural Greece, these organizations view technology as a tool for enabling communities to autonomously shape their futures, free from external pressures such as market demands or ideological influences. In this way, technology becomes a means of political contestation and self-determination rather than a neutral instrument.

The second dimension refers to the resources that organizations require or exploit to function. As Polanyi (2001) observed, industrial capitalism achieved its growth by transforming traditional arrangements involving land and labour into marketable commodities, subjecting them to economic transactions and calculations. Growth-oriented organizations continue to perpetuate this logic by appropriating common resource pools (for example, water, land, natural resources, public goods) and labour (Mattei, 2011; Rätzer et al, 2018). In essence, economic growth relies on the appropriation and commodification of previously communal goods (Martinez-Alier, 2002; Kallis, 2018). When the appropriation of material resources reaches its limits, growth progresses by commodifying various aspects of social life in increasingly sophisticated ways. Examples include the privatization of care, healthcare, education, knowledge, and the establishment of intellectual property regimes (Conde and Walter, 2015;

Gomez-Baggethun, 2015). Contrary to this trend, post growth-oriented organizations resist commodification across many sectors. For instance, grassroots movements in the Global North advocate for autonomy in determining the type of energy and food they consume and how these are produced. Most of the cases presented (for example, grassroots innovation and appropriate technology cases) above often emphasize non-market solutions, such as exchange or self-production. Social cooperatives underscore the significance of non-marketized care systems that operate outside the profit-driven logic of the market (Poledrini, 2014; Pansera and Rizzi, 2020). Additionally, knowledge is frequently treated as a form of commons within these initiatives, fostering collaboration and sharing rather than exclusion (Hess and Ostrom, 2007). For example, intellectual property regimes, which commodify knowledge, are often ignored by appropriate technology organizations, challenged by the STN, and circumvented through alternative open licenses in open and collaborative production settings, such as the P2P Lab in Greece, fab labs, makerspaces, and open-source communities (Hielscher and Smith, 2014).

Another key characteristic of post growth-oriented organizations is their ownership and governance structures, which often prioritize worker-owned models and horizontal management approaches. In contrast, growth-oriented organizations typically adhere to traditional hierarchical structures, such as the pyramidal systems found in multinational corporations, where control is concentrated in private boards and shareholders. Ownership and governance structures directly influence the production and consumption patterns within organizations. Growth-oriented organizations are often export-driven and operate on a global scale, adhering to a geographical and social division of labour designed to minimize labour costs and environmental compliance while maximizing profits. This model frequently results in a disconnect between production and consumption processes

(Gouveia and Juska, 2002; Ritzer and Jurgenson, 2010). Conversely, post growth organizations emphasize local markets and consumption networks. In many cases analysed within the STN in Brazil, production and consumption overlap – for instance, producers and consumers are often the same individuals. This overlap is also evident in collaborative production systems; for example, Linux developers are also its primary users. Another notable feature of post growth organizations is their efforts to involve consumers in decision-making processes related to production. These organizations aspire to align production with the values and worldviews of consumers rather than dictating consumer preferences based on production goals (Anderson, 2012).

One of the most notable differences between growth-oriented and post growth organizations lies in how they manage surplus. As Romano (2015) argues, patterns of surplus utilization have historically defined and distinguished different types of human groups across space and time. In growth-oriented organizations, surplus is typically reinvested to enhance total factor productivity or distributed as dividends to shareholders. As previously discussed, Piketty (2014) highlights how increases in factor productivity since the 1970s have been distributed unevenly between labour and capital. This disparity coincided with the neoliberal shift in the global economy and the decline of union bargaining power in nearly all industrialized countries (Western, 1995). This trend has significantly hindered the development of democratic mechanisms for deciding how surplus should be reinvested. In contrast, the management of surplus in post growth organizations is often less straightforward. One reason is that many such organizations struggle to survive and rarely generate significant surplus. However, in cases like social cooperatives, surplus can be either reinvested to improve productivity or redistributed among cooperative members. Importantly, decisions regarding surplus reinvestment tend to be made democratically.

As previously mentioned, intellectual property is strongly opposed by most of the post growth organizations presented above. Property rights are often framed as a form of commodification and a barrier to the free exchange of knowledge (Bollier, 2008; May, 2015). This perspective aligns closely with the vision of technological development held by post growth advocates, who tend to favour decentralized and distributed forms of technology design over expert-driven innovation (Kerschner et al, 2018). Many examples of post growth organizations reflect the principles of convivial technologies, as conceptualized by Illich (1973). In the cases we analysed, these characteristics are particularly prominent in militant organizations, often based on the principles of common-based peer productions, like the P2P Lab, CoopCycle, and, more generally, in the makers and fab labs communities.

While growth-oriented organizations often view innovation as a process of continuous novelty creation, post growth proponents see technology as a tool for social emancipation – a vehicle with a normative direction shaped through collective participation (Stirling, 2008). This perspective invites a broader debate on how technological development and innovation shape and restructure power relationships within society. Growth-oriented organizations – especially multinational corporations in sectors like fossil fuels, pharmaceuticals, and agro-food – often operate beyond the reach of democratic control. They frequently engage with democratic institutions through technocratic and opaque decision-making processes that are inaccessible to the public. The secrecy surrounding negotiations for agreements such as the Transatlantic Trade and Investment Partnership, the Comprehensive Economic and Trade Agreement, and the Trade in Services Agreement is a classic example (War on Want, 2015). Consequently, technological and innovation-related decisions in these contexts tend to favour growth-oriented organizations while marginalizing alternative approaches or debates. In contrast, post growth organizations typically operate within local social networks, far removed from centres of political and economic power. Many explicitly challenge dominant power structures in pursuit of social emancipation and autonomy (Smith and Ely, 2015).

Another key distinction lies in the scale of operation. Growth-oriented organizations are characterized by large-scale production aimed at reducing costs and diversifying products, often leading to the formation of aggregations and oligopolies. Post growth organizations, on the other hand, adopt a more nuanced approach to scaling. As Colombo et al (2023) highlight, scaling in post growth organizations encompasses a diverse range of strategies beyond traditional organizational growth. In the context of Italian social agricultural cooperatives, nine distinct scaling routes were identified, including organizational growth (both vertical and horizontal), organizational downscaling, policy impact, multiplication, cultural impact (both organizational and societal), aggregation, and diffusion. This research emphasizes that post growth scaling: (1) requires the synergistic interaction of multiple strategies, (2) prioritizes influencing societal culture, (3) does not inherently depend on organizational growth, and (4) is embedded within socio-ecological systems as a relational process. For instance, grassroots movements often replicate their models through knowledge exchange and collaboration with other groups, while social cooperatives focus on multiplication and replication over expansion to safeguard internal democratic processes (Kasmir, 1999). Similarly, open and collaborative production models exemplify flexibility and distributed organizational structures, which can be rapidly reconfigured to adapt to specific contingencies (Weber, 2005; Benkler, 2016). This broader typology of scaling routes empowers post growth organizations to unlock their transformative potential, advancing a vision of economic systems oriented towards human and ecological flourishing.

Towards a new approach to post growth organization studies

The various approaches to non-growth-oriented innovation – such as appropriate technology, grassroots movements, social cooperatives, and open-source production – offer significant and compelling alternatives to the dominant frameworks that prioritize economic growth. Despite their differences in focus and application, these approaches share a commitment to decentralization, local autonomy, and the democratization of knowledge and resources. By fostering inclusive and context-sensitive innovation practices, they directly challenge the economic and social imperatives of growth. Instead, they present a vision of development that emphasizes social equity, environmental sustainability, and community empowerment. Through their focus on participation, distributed knowledge, and non-proprietary solutions, these frameworks illustrate how innovation can transcend traditional growth paradigms, paving the way for more resilient and equitable futures. The examples discussed above reveal that alternative ways of framing innovation are not scarce. In fact, the study of these alternative modes of innovation highlights several research implications that require further attention.

First, it becomes apparent that post growth-oriented innovations often emerge from organizations that closely align with Gibson-Graham's (2006) concept of community and alternative economies. Gibson-Graham identifies mainstream market capitalism as growth-oriented, while alternative economies are described as 'vitality-oriented'. These alternative forms create diversity within the economic landscape and simultaneously challenge the hegemonic, capitalocentric dynamics of growth, accumulation, commodification, and centralization – mechanisms that underpin capitalism's dominance and its perception as natural and inevitable. This suggests that innovation and technological change in a post growth economy would likely require fundamental questioning of the capitalist forms of production, consumption, and the political and scientific institutions built around this model. However, it remains unclear whether science, technology, and innovation in a post growth era can be compatible with modified versions of dominant organizational forms – such as firms, multinational corporations, nation-states, or universities – or if these changes would require a radical transformation of such institutions. In either scenario, the precise nature and modalities of this transformation demand deeper investigation. This transformation appears particularly hard when we observe that, historically, the biggest scientific and technological efforts were founded to serve military interests to achieve geopolitical strategic goals. The space race or the development of microelectronics are famous examples of this dynamic. It is reasonable to think that our scientific institutions are inevitably intertwined with imperialism and militarism? Can they be transformed? By whom? Is it a feasible project or do we rather build new institutions from the scratch?

Second, it is evident that post growth or even degrowth strategies in many alternative innovation efforts are often the unintended outcomes of opposing how technological development is managed and governed rather than deliberate attempts to reject economic growth altogether. Alternative organizational forms do not generally reject science and technology outright but seek to reorient them towards solving social needs without mandating economic growth as a necessary outcome. Furthermore, some alternative organizations may pursue certain forms of growth, such as expanding memberships, clients, knowledge bases, or technological solutions. For instance, cooperatives like the Mondragon Corporation in Spain exemplify how such organizations can operate within growth-oriented paradigms while maintaining their alternative principles (Storey et al, 2014).

Third, while collaborative value creation and the technologies that enable it align with post growth objectives, they do not inherently guarantee the realization of those objectives. Similarly, workplace democracy, coproduction, and work-time reduction, though compatible with post growth ideals, do not necessarily lead to a post growth society. Additionally, the cases of companies like Uber and Airbnb illustrate how concepts associated with social, alternative, or community economies are constantly at risk of co-optation and exploitation by growth-oriented organizations seeking novel profit opportunities (Martin, 2016). These dynamics underscore the need for a coherent theoretical framework that links currently fragmented concepts, such as democracy, participation, responsibility, environmental sustainability, social justice, and power dynamics, in the study of alternative modes of innovation.

Fourth, the examples of alternative innovation approaches highlight the importance of addressing issues related to scale, ownership, and the direction of technological and innovation systems. For instance, appropriate technologies have demonstrated that downscaling technologies is critical for achieving local autonomy and control. In contrast, grassroots innovation movements emphasize the importance of scaling applications while retaining control over knowledge and technologies to meet the basic needs of larger populations. Digital open and collaborative initiatives focus on increasing knowledge production and innovation to create collective solutions, challenging traditional economic firms (Benkler, 2016). These varied approaches demonstrate that there is no single path forwards; each model frames issues of scale, ownership, and knowledge production differently. What becomes evident is the centrality of epistemological plurality – a space where diverse sources of knowledge, including scientific, local, indigenous, and community-based knowledge, can coexist. Integrating this diversity within current institutions for science, technology, and innovation represents a significant and underexplored challenge.

FIVE

The Infrastructural Conditions of Post Growth

'Socialism can only arrive by bicycle', Chilean socialist politician José Antonio Viera Gallo once said (Riechmann, 2022). The bicycle has become an icon of the degrowth movement: simple, efficient, and quietly revolutionary. It promises low-impact mobility without the noise, cost, or CO_2 emissions of the car. Ivan Illich, an early proponent of degrowth, famously praised bicycles not just for their low-energy demands but for embodying the values of autonomy and simplicity – principles at the heart of the degrowth movement. Decades later, Jason Hickel (2023) echoed this sentiment in his reflection on the role of technology in degrowth: '… sometimes simpler technologies are more effective, more efficient, and more democratic: bicycles, for instance, are an incredibly powerful technology for helping to decarbonize urban transport'.

From a degrowth perspective, it's not hard to see the appeal. They are relatively affordable compared to cars, require minimal energy input (beyond human effort); they are also durable and, depending on the type, relatively easy to repair and maintain. Bicycles are compatible with slow living, and their use can foster a sense of community and physical well-being. They allegedly break from our dependency on huge infrastructures, like highways, airports, or railways. Bicycles can slip through traffic, connect neighbourhoods, and bring cities back to a human scale. Riding one feels like a quiet act of resistance – against sprawl, speed, and the steel dominance of the car. In the degrowth imagination, the bicycle is more than a machine. It's a blueprint for another way of living. However, this framing, while compelling, risks veering into a form of technological determinism – the assumption that the widespread adoption of bicycles will inherently lead to a sustainable, equitable, and post growth society. This oversimplification fails to address the broader systems in which technologies, including bicycles, are embedded.

Bicycles alone won't lead to a post growth society

Technologies never exist in isolation. They are always part of broader systems involving production, design, distribution, knowledge, and social relations. What technologies do – and how they affect society – depends on these systems and the power relations embedded in them (Winner, 1978). The bicycle, often idealized as a paradigmatic degrowth technology, is no exception. The manufacturing of a modern bicycle is a complex process that spans global supply chains. An average bicycle might be assembled using components manufactured in over ten countries, relying on intricate systems of production and logistics. The rise of electric bicycles (e-bikes), while expanding the accessibility of cycling to new demographics, has introduced additional layers of complexity, particularly through the use of lithium-ion batteries. The production of these batteries involves mining and processing rare earth materials, a practice often associated with significant environmental, old and new colonial forms of exploitation and their associated social costs. While e-bikes may facilitate mobility in hilly or long-distance scenarios, their value chains illustrate the embeddedness of bicycles within globalized and resource-intensive systems.

Far from egalitarian, bicycles have also become sites of conspicuous consumption. High-end bikes, cycling gear, and accessories often serve as markers of class, taste, and lifestyle – more about aesthetic distinction than ecological commitment. Once inserted in these competitive logics, the pressure to upgrade equipment often mirrors the same consumerist impulses degrowth seeks to overcome. There are other ways in which bicycles can reproduce social hierarchies. For example, in many urban settings, cycling infrastructure disproportionately benefits affluent neighbourhoods, while low-income communities are left navigating car-dominated environments with higher safety risks. Furthermore, bicycles are not universally accessible. Individuals with physical disabilities, for example, may find bicycles unsuitable for their mobility needs. While adaptive cycles and tricycles exist, they are often less readily available and more expensive. Geographic and climatic factors also pose challenges. Bicycles may work well in flat, temperate cities but are less practical in hilly terrain or rainy or extreme weather conditions. These limitations highlight the need for a diverse array of mobility solutions rather than a singular focus on bicycles.

A takeaway from this is that, when it comes to technology, simplicity is rarely simple. What looks effortless – riding a bicycle, say – is often just the polished tip of a vast and hidden machinery: materials mined continents away (often by underpaid racialized miners), carefully engineered components, supply chains that stretch across oceans, knowledge built over generations, and cultural narratives that shape how we use and value the apparatus. We tend to think of simplicity and complexity as opposites. But more often, simplicity is what complexity looks like once it's been buried out of sight. The focus on individual technologies or single artefacts risks obscuring the deeper socio-technical complexity at play – and with it, the scale of the transformation required. A truly democratic and sustainable post growth society will demand more than elegant tools. It will require a far-reaching reconfiguration of production and consumption systems, infrastructures, and the social relations that hold them together.

THE INFRASTRUCTURAL CONDITIONS OF POST GROWTH

When it comes to grappling with the question of technological complexity for post growth, the role of infrastructure emerges as an ideal site. As we argued elsewhere (Pansera et al, 2024), infrastructure is a critical yet underexplored aspect of post growth scholarship. Many degrowth/post growth scholars argue that high levels of societal well-being can be maintained in a non-growing economy, but this requires a radical transformation of existing consumption and production arrangements. Infrastructure, as the foundation of modern societies, plays a central role in this transformation. Reliable systems for clean energy, water, sanitation, mobility, and communication are prerequisites for achieving material well-being in a sustainable manner. However, these systems are often deeply intertwined with economic growth paradigms. The bicycle, as a tool, depends on infrastructure to be produced, distributed, and effectively used. Dedicated bike lanes, safe storage facilities, and repair workshops are essential components of a bicycle-friendly environment. Without these, bicycles may remain an underutilized or inaccessible option for many. Likewise, the production and maintenance of bicycles depend on industrial and logistical infrastructures embedded within the global economy, often intertwined with both historical and contemporary forms of colonial extractivism. Addressing these interconnected systems is crucial for ensuring that bicycles can contribute meaningfully to a post growth society.

While bicycles embody many of the ideals of the degrowth movement, they shouldn't be viewed as a panacea for the challenges of transitioning to a sustainable and equitable future. Instead, they should be considered as one piece of a much larger puzzle. Post growth scholarship must go beyond the simplistic idea that any single technology can solve systemic problems. It requires a nuanced understanding of how technologies interact with social, economic, and environmental systems. This calls for a shift in focus from individual technologies to the systems that support and sustain them. How can production systems be reconfigured to reduce their environmental and social impact?

What kinds of infrastructure are needed to support sustainable mobility? How can social relations be transformed to prioritize well-being over consumption? What do we do with the present infrastructures, such as nuclear plants, military complexes, fossil fuel facilities, that are incompatible with post growth imaginaries? These are the questions that need to be addressed. The challenges of building a post growth society require systemic change that goes far beyond the adoption of any single technology. Recognizing the complexity of technological systems and their integration into societal structures is essential for crafting effective strategies for change. Post growth and degrowth scholarship must grapple with these complexities to ensure that the transition to a sustainable and equitable society is both comprehensive and inclusive. This implies, as Durrant and Cohen (2024) suggest, putting a democratic governance of infrastructures at the centre of post growth politics and potential post growth policies proposals. By doing so, we can move beyond the bicycle as a symbol and towards a deeper understanding of the systems that shape our world.

The social construction of infrastructure

The uncomfortable truth about the systemic nature of technology is that, once large technological systems are deployed and widely accepted, they possess a tremendous inertia. This fact is extremely relevant when our task is to reconfigure technology to enable a post growth society. In his seminal essay, 'Do Artifacts Have Politics?', Langdon Winner (1980) illustrates the ways in which infrastructures can constrain social possibilities and entrench power dynamics within society. Winner discusses the construction of overpasses on Long Island by Robert Moses, a public official responsible for much of New York's infrastructural expansion from the 1920s to the 1970s. Winner argues that Moses designed these overpasses to prevent public buses from passing underneath, thereby limiting access to public parks and beaches for working-class and non-white New Yorkers. Through such infrastructure, Winner posits, Moses embedded his own racist and classist prejudices into the physical environment, with the intent of maintaining these social divisions long after his departure. This notion of 'doing politics' through urban technology and infrastructure underscores the perspective within STS that technology and society are mutually constitutive. Although Winner's example of Long Island bridges has faced criticism and debate in subsequent decades regarding the extent to which infrastructural intentions shape function (Joerges, 1999; Rowland and Passoth, 2015), there is broad consensus within science and technology scholars about urban infrastructure's potential to either enable or constrain social possibilities. Similar cases of in-built biases can be found in many other sectors. In their first tests, the Google driverless cars were unable to avoid Black people because their facial recognition algorithms were trained by white programmers who used only pictures of white individuals.[1] As we discussed in Chapter 2, technology usually embeds the values of its designer often unintentionally. This raises critical questions about the extent to which other embedded assumptions, such as perpetual growth, are similarly inscribed within infrastructural systems. If the imaginaries of our engineers, designers, and planners are shaped by a society that praises economic growth and expansion as the ultimate value, it is reasonable to think that the technological systems they create are designed to enable such an expansion. This is not something limited to a discursive or ideological level. This is something directly inscribed in the materiality of our daily life, in the way we commute, in the ways we produce our food and in the way we spend our leisure time. If this is true, it easy to see how replacing cars with bicycles can't be a way to degrowth.

Any democratic initiative to downscale the economy, particularly in the Global North, must contend with the dominance of technological utopianism within growth-centric societies. Growth-oriented institutions project technological futures onto the socio-technical imaginaries that guide and justify infrastructure production (Jasanoff and Kim, 2015; Kerschner et al, 2018). If growth is indeed embedded in the material structures of contemporary societies, as we suggest, changing societal values alone may be insufficient to achieve a democratic planned degrowth. As Shove and Trentmann (2018) highlight, the physical and symbolic presence of infrastructure – ranging from pylons and highways to sewage systems and electric grids – embodies growth. Nevertheless, these systems are often overlooked in post growth narratives that prioritize localized actions and technologies. Consequently, alongside shifts in collective imagination, post growth scholarship and activists must also consider two underexplored areas: the relationship of post growth thinking with technology and the question of scale.

Post growth thinking, convivial technology, and the question of scale

As we already pointed out in the previous chapters, a significant influence on contemporary degrowth scholarship in the realm of technology has been the work of Ivan Illich. Illich's ideas are rooted in a key distinction between democratic and authoritarian infrastructures. He argued for the necessity of greater autonomy – freedom from the grip of large-scale technological infrastructures and the centralized bureaucratic institutions, whether public or private, that control them. To achieve this, Illich introduced the concept of convivial tools: technologies designed to empower individuals and communities while avoiding the hierarchies and dominance of non-democratic, large-scale techno-structures. His seminal work in 1973 remains foundational in degrowth debates, advocating for technologies that are accessible, manageable, and promote self-reliance rather than dependency. In recent years, scholars have revisited Illich's critique, seeking to explore the complex and often contradictory relationship between degrowth and technology. This exploration has highlighted what some describe as a 'love/hate' dynamic. On the one hand, there is recognition of the potential for democratized technologies to align with degrowth principles; on the other hand, there is scepticism about how deeply intertwined many technologies remain with growth-driven systems. Two key areas of focus have emerged: the need to democratize technology and the importance of revisiting how technologies are governed and assessed. Practical examples of democratized technologies often emerge from small-scale experiments – sometimes referred to as 'nowtopias' – like ecovillages based on appropriate low-tech technologies, energy communities, and other grassroots initiatives. These experiments provide valuable real-world insights into what a degrowth future might look like when democratic technologies take centre stage. However, while these small-scale initiatives are inspiring, their impact remains limited. They exist on the fringes, both within the societies that host them and as a share of the vast infrastructural systems that dominate the planet. While they demonstrate that alternatives to the current growth-oriented models are theoretically possible, they have yet to prove their capacity to scale up or replace the entrenched global systems that underpin much of modern life. Thus, while such experiments generate hope and offer critical lessons, they serve more as starting points for imagining alternative futures than as definitive solutions to the challenges posed by authoritarian and hierarchical infrastructures.

As we argued in Chapter 2, the field of STS plays a vital role in bridging the gap between society, technology and infrastructure, offering a nuanced understanding of their deeply intertwined relationship. Science and technology studies emphasize the co-productive dynamic between technology and social systems, showing how each shape and is shaped by the other. With a rich history of exploring large socio-technical systems, such as electricity grids, as demonstrated in Hughes' (1993) seminal work, this scholarship provides valuable insights into how such systems evolve and function. More recent contributions by STS-influenced scholars, such as Geels (2002, 2005), have further enriched this body of knowledge, shedding light on the complex network of social relations, material factors, and human and non-human actors that govern the transformation of small-scale technologies into large-scale infrastructures.

This perspective is particularly significant given how much of the post growth and degrowth literature tend to overlook the role of existing infrastructural networks. Too often, technology is misinterpreted as merely material and inanimate, divorced from the socio-political and economic systems that shape its development and use. As Serres (1995) shows, these networks form the material foundation of our world, embedding legacies of historical relationships – both between and within states – and, critically, between human society and the natural world. For post growth thinking to move beyond its current position on the fringes of mainstream discourse, it must engage seriously with this reality. Doing so would help address criticisms that post growth and degrowth are anti-modern or opposed to technological innovation, enabling the movement to present a more nuanced and actionable vision of sustainable progress. A critical misstep in some degrowth thinking is the assumption that all technologies envisioned under degrowth scenarios must necessarily be small scale. In reality, transformative shifts, such as the transition to a circular economy and the large-scale adoption of renewable energy, are compatible with and central to the restructuring of economies in a degrowth/post growth framework. These shifts require a careful analysis of which sectors should expand and which should contract, emphasizing resource efficiency and sustainability at the scale of national and international economies (Hardt et al, 2021).

The challenges of addressing issues beyond the local scale have been acknowledged by several degrowth scholars, who critique the way early influences, such as Serge Latouche, uncritically accepted a rigid distinction between the local, national, and global scales. Discussions of technology within the degrowth framework are often informed by this oversimplified interpretation of scale, where the local is not only assumed to be inherently superior but also idealized as the optimal scale for transformative change (Lloveras et al, 2021). This idealization, or what some scholars describe as a 'fetishization of the local', is particularly evident in the emphasis placed on small-scale technologies as inherently aligned with degrowth values (Kallis and March, 2015). However, focusing solely on the local or small-scale level limits the degrowth discourse, neglecting the potential for systemic change that integrates larger-scale processes. Emerging pathways are beginning to challenge this narrow focus, offering alternatives that combine the strengths of localism with broader scalability. One such pathway is replication, which Pansera and Fressoli (2021) propose as a way to avoid the centralization and oligopolistic tendencies that often arise in large-scale systems. Replication involves creating multiple, smaller, interconnected systems rather than expanding a single, monolithic structure. This approach not only mitigates the risk of over-centralization but also promotes internal democracy within systems. Similar strategies have been observed by Colombo et al (2023) in the case of social cooperatives that present a variety of scaling patterns. None of them implies to exclusively restrict their activities to their local environments. The principles of replication echo Ebenezer Howard's polycentric model of urban development, proposed in 1965. Howard envisioned communities designed to remain within an ideal size, establishing new settlements as populations grew beyond a certain threshold. This approach maintains a balance between scalability and liveability, ensuring that growth does not come at the expense of autonomy or community cohesion. Similarly, recent efforts to apply degrowth principles to urban planning have embraced the idea of autonomy at a regional scale. For example, the notion of degrowth circularity proposed by Savini (2019) highlights the potential for regional autonomy to combine local self-reliance with broader, interconnected planning frameworks, aligning degrowth values with practical, scalable solutions.

Expanding the focus beyond small-scale technologies reveals promising pathways for degrowth, and post growth thinking more in general, to address the challenges of scale. These approaches illustrate that systemic transformation does not require an outright rejection of large-scale processes. Instead, it involves reimagining how these processes are organized, governed, and replicated to align with the principles of sustainability, democracy, and equity. Variations on this idea are evident in the growing body of work on degrowth and innovation. Scholars like Vetter (2018) and Pansera and Fressoli (2021) highlight modularity as a key approach to distinguishing convivial technologies from those driven by growth-oriented imperatives. While modularity is often discussed in mainstream critiques of large-scale infrastructures as a tool for upscaling, degrowth perspectives emphasize the importance of modularity for downscaling as well. This reframing shifts the focus from building ever-larger systems to creating adaptable, decentralized networks that can scale down when necessary. The digital technology sector provides compelling examples of this principle in action. Open-source technologies, such as Wikipedia and Linux, operate effectively at scale while maintaining collaborative, non-hierarchical structures. Despite challenges in implementation, including gender imbalances and issues of inclusivity, these examples demonstrate the feasibility of managing complex systems without relying on centralized control. This insight is critical for how degrowth thinking begins to engage more productively with the question of scale. Open-source technologies and modular systems challenge the assumption that complex infrastructures must always be hierarchical or that large-scale management is inherently incompatible with democratic principles. It provides contemporary examples to support a body of evidence that questions the assumption that the management of complex infrastructures is inherently hierarchical and only achievable at the large scale (Graeber and Wengrow, 2021).

For a degrowth vision to have a realistic chance of success, it is essential to explore how a planned contraction of the economy might function in practice, particularly at the scale required to sustain complex infrastructures like the internet. This brings the issue of infrastructure sharply into focus. As previously mentioned, addressing the question of infrastructure solely at the local scale remains within the comfort zone of degrowth but falls short of engaging with the broader systemic challenges. Limiting the discussion to local governance risks perpetuating false assumptions that democratic governance is inherently tied to small scales, overlooking the need for solutions that span urban, national, and global levels. Expanding the conversation to the urban scale introduces valuable real-world examples of commons-based and publicly governed infrastructures. These instances demonstrate the potential for rethinking infrastructure governance beyond profit-driven models. However, even at the urban level, too much ground is often ceded to large-scale, state-led, and market-driven projects. These projects frequently reflect the priorities of elites and entrenched power structures, relying heavily on state backing to maintain their operations. This dynamic is particularly problematic in contexts where states are either too weak or too deeply intertwined with global infrastructure industries to act in the public interest. The power embedded in infrastructure itself becomes a critical point of contention. As argued by The Invisible Committee (The Invisible Committee, 2017), modern infrastructure has evolved into a locus of power, influencing societal organization and economic systems on a massive scale. Multi-trillion-dollar programs aimed at addressing global 'infrastructure gaps' exemplify this dynamic. While these programs are often framed as essential to achieving sustainable development goals, they are fundamentally embedded in a growth paradigm. Their primary objective is not to create equitable or sustainable systems but to expand infrastructure capacity to meet the demands of projected economic growth. Such framing positions sustainability as an additional cost, requiring even greater investment, rather than as a guiding principle for reimagining infrastructure. For degrowth to confront these entrenched dynamics, it must move beyond the narrow confines of localism and develop strategies that address the systemic power imbalances inherent in large-scale infrastructure systems. Only by doing so can degrowth offer a meaningful alternative to the growth-oriented frameworks that dominate contemporary infrastructure planning and governance.

Are our infrastructures designed to grow?

To meaningfully experiment with democratic governance of mega-infrastructures, post growth thinkers must first understand how such infrastructures emerge and how the values and ideologies of growth become embedded within them. The consolidation and expansion of material infrastructures is a complex and dynamic process, one that demands an appreciation of historical, socio-economic, and technical intricacies. These intricacies are best understood through a synthesis of science, technology, and society studies and the works of scholars like Geels et al (2002, 2016) and Hughes (1993). While Geels focuses on technological regime transitions, Hughes delves into the development of large technological systems. Together, their insights reveal the interplay of forces that shape modern infrastructures. Infrastructures can be seen as embedded within broader socio-technical landscapes. These landscapes are not static; they are legacies of historical processes involving multiple temporal layers and constant reconfigurations of earlier arrangements. As Geels (2002) explains, these landscapes encompass more than just physical entities like cities, factories, highways, and electricity grids. They also include a diverse array of factors – ranging from oil prices and economic growth to wars, migration, political coalitions, cultural norms, and environmental challenges – that collectively shape actor interactions within these systems.

The socio-technical landscape within which modern infrastructures have emerged is deeply intertwined with the growth paradigm. This paradigm reflects the gradual alignment of state and private interests around the idea that economic growth is the ultimate societal goal. At its core, the growth paradigm is driven by three interrelated factors (Pansera et al, 2024). First, there is the widespread acceptance of economic growth as a supreme aspiration, bolstered by the use of metrics like GDP as the primary measure of societal progress. Second, this paradigm necessitates the relentless pursuit of new energy sources and technological innovations to expand society's metabolic flows – essentially, its capacity to process and consume energy and materials – leading to increased surpluses of energy and matter. Finally, the paradigm relies on the establishment of social relationships rooted in private property, social class divisions, and the pursuit of profit maximization. These institutionalized logics of growth not only shape societal values but also dictate the trajectory of infrastructure development. They create environments where expansion is not just possible but expected, reinforcing a feedback loop that prioritizes scale and efficiency over sustainability and equity. Understanding these dynamics is crucial for post growth scholars seeking to disrupt the deeply entrenched systems that sustain growth-dependent infrastructures. By doing so, they can begin to envision and advocate for alternative pathways that align with democratic governance, environmental stewardship, and social well-being.

Geels (2002, 2016) introduces the concept of landscapes to explain the evolution of technological regimes. These landscapes represent the intricate web of interactions among social actors, markets, social institutions, and cultural forces that collectively shape the trajectory of technological systems. Hughes (1993, 2004), by contrast, focuses specifically on the development of large technical systems, such as the electrification networks in Europe and the United States. Hughes investigates the factors driving the growth of these systems, offering valuable insights into how infrastructure projects transition from initial flexibility and openness to entrenched patterns of expansion within a capitalist framework. Hughes demonstrates that during their early stages, infrastructure projects often feature diverse designs, purposes, and technological possibilities. However, as these projects mature, they become increasingly locked into patterns of growth, shaped by both technological and economic imperatives. A prime example of this dynamic is the development of electric grids in industrialized nations. On the technological side, the expansion of these grids was largely driven by the need to maximize the load factor – a key metric defined as the average load of electricity divided by the peak load over a specified period (Hughes, 1993). Ensuring a high load factor was essential for the economic viability of electricity distribution systems, prompting efforts to electrify productive activities, such as factories, public buildings, and transportation networks. To further improve efficiency and cost-effectiveness, high-voltage transmission lines were strategically deployed to connect diverse energy sources like hydropower and coal. This approach created complementary networks that leveraged the geographic diversity of energy resources, ultimately reducing electricity prices and increasing accessibility. Hughes (1993, p 463) succinctly captures this dynamic, stating:

> Whereas load factor considerations led utilities to exploit the diversity of human geography, economic mix dictated expansion to exploit the diversity of natural geography [...] The decisions made to improve load factor and economic mix shaped the growing electric supply systems in their cost-accounting settings.

In essence, Hughes shows how these systems were designed not only to meet immediate technical demands but also to align with broader economic objectives, creating a feedback loop that reinforced their expansion. The system's technical and economic viability was fundamentally tied to its capacity for continuous expansion. Any attempt to reverse or halt this growth model would introduce significant challenges for existing grids. The interplay between economic and technical factors created what Hughes describes as technological momentum – a self-reinforcing force that drives the expansion of infrastructure and solidifies existing technological regimes. This momentum ensures that once a system is established, it becomes increasingly difficult to deviate from its trajectory. This phenomenon is further elaborated by Winner (2004), who used the term 'technological somnambulism' to describe society's tendency to uncritically adopt and perpetuate existing technologies without fully considering their long-term consequences. This unexamined reliance on established systems fosters a kind of inertia, making it exceedingly difficult for alternative, more sustainable solutions to gain traction. The entrenched nature of such infrastructures not only perpetuates growth-oriented paradigms but also limits society's ability to envision and implement transformative changes that prioritize sustainability and equity over expansion. This locking-in of infrastructure growth underscores the deep interconnection between technological innovation and the economic logics of capitalism, raising critical questions about how such systems can be reimagined within alternative, non-growth-oriented frameworks.

The internet, with its vast network of submarine cables, data centres spanning continents, and satellite links, one of the most extensive global infrastructures, is an emblematic example of this dynamic (Blum, 2012). Paradoxically, it remains largely invisible to its five billion users, who primarily interact with terminal devices like laptops or smartphones. These devices mask the immense hardware systems enabling streaming, gaming, and sharing photos in the cloud. Far from being an immaterial utopia, the internet relies on a massive physical infrastructure intertwined with flows of energy, material resources, geographic territories, and even the biosphere – what Bratton (2016) refers to as 'the stack'. Unlike traditional industrial infrastructures, the internet did not arise from a unified master plan. While some foundational components were the result of deliberate scientific efforts, its current form is a product of converging technologies shaped by complex technical and social interactions across scales and histories. This emergent order reflects an unmanaged, unplanned evolution, making the internet a unique case study in the dynamics of global infrastructures.

The internet has been a driving force behind economic growth over the past three decades, fuelling the rapid expansion of digital technology, the fastest-growing sector in the global economy. But this raises an important question: Is this vast, planetary infrastructure designed to expand indefinitely, or is it locked into a growth-dependent path due to its physical and institutional structures? To understand this, it helps to analyse the internet on two levels: its physical layer – the hardware and software that enable its functionality – and its logical layer, which governs its operations through protocols, rules, and policies (Frischmann, 2005).

The physical layer includes submarine cables, data centres, landlines, radio links, and satellites, as well as the devices we interact with, like phones and computers (Pansera et al, 2024). Contrary to popular belief, satellites are not the primary enablers of global internet connectivity; instead, 99 per cent of data flows through an extensive network of undersea cables. These cables, which trace their origins to nineteenth-century telegraph networks, now form a global web, meeting an ever-growing demand for bandwidth. Since 2016, cable capacity has doubled every two years. In recent years, tech giants like Amazon, Google, and Meta have started funding their own private submarine cables to bypass traditional carriers and gain direct control over their data traffic. For example, Google's Dunant cable, launched in 2020, can transmit the entire digital content of the US Library of Congress three times per second. These investments, amounting to billions of dollars, are driven by the need for greater bandwidth to store and process vast amounts of data. Submarine cables are designed to handle disruptions like earthquakes or ship anchors, and they often have over-dimensioned bandwidth to prepare for future demand. This over-dimensioning reduces the need for immediate upgrades but perpetuates the cycle of expansion. Rather than increasing the capacity of existing cables, companies often lay new ones, which are cheaper, more advanced, and more scalable. Another critical part of the physical layer is data centres – massive facilities that store, process, and transfer information. These centres are the 'engines' of the internet, consuming vast amounts of energy and accounting for a significant share of its carbon footprint. Tech giants like Amazon, Google, and Meta, which own many data centres, also dominate internet traffic, collectively generating over half of the world's broadband activity. To ensure resilience, data centres use backup systems and replicate their operations across multiple locations. This flexibility comes at a cost, as redundancy drives exponential growth in data centre capacity and energy consumption. In addition to human-driven demand, the internet increasingly accommodates non-human users, such as bots, sensors, and smart devices. Automated traffic now makes up 64 per cent of all internet activity, a figure that includes legitimate uses, like AI, and malicious activities, such as hacking. As more devices connect to the internet and data grows, so does the energy and material consumption required to support this expansion. The result is a system that feeds its own growth, increasing emissions and environmental impact rather than dematerializing the economy. For instance, data centres alone are projected to account for nearly half of the ICT sector's global greenhouse gas emissions by 2040, as their energy demands skyrocket (Pansera et al, 2024).

Although the internet's physical infrastructure was not explicitly designed to grow indefinitely, its evolution reflects inherent growth incentives tied to both its physical and logical layers. This 'growth dependency' stems from how these layers are structured and operated. Initially conceived as a flexible and scalable network, the internet has developed through clusters of unplanned and unmanaged infrastructures. However, technological advancements, especially in electronics and telecommunications, have fuelled exponential innovation, setting expectations for faster speeds, greater bandwidth, and continuous upgrades. In the physical layer, over-dimensioned designs, like fiber-optic cables and routers, are built for future capacity rather than current demand. This overcapacity, combined with advancements in fiber-optic technology, encourages perpetual growth, catering to both human users and an increasing share of non-human traffic, such as bots and AI systems. Meanwhile, private ownership of critical infrastructure, such as submarine cables and data centres, intensifies this growth dynamic. Companies like Amazon, Google, and Meta push for expanded network capacity to meet the demands of AI, big data, and video streaming, all of which require vast amounts of computational power and energy. The business models of these tech giants rely on accumulating user data, creating a feedback loop where more data fuels more growth.

The logical layer of the internet, which governs how its systems operate, is another critical factor. This layer includes protocols and rules that ensure interoperability and scalability. While these systems were designed to allow flexibility and even downscaling in theory, in practice, they are optimized for continuous growth. For example, protocols like IPv6 can accommodate exponentially more devices than are currently connected,[2] ensuring the internet's infrastructure remains ready to support future expansion. Over-dimensioning is also common at this level, as companies design systems to handle peak traffic, similar to the dynamics of expansion of the electric grids described by Hughes, and reduce the need for frequent upgrades. Ultimately, the internet's growth is deeply embedded in the competitive global economy, where companies expect ever-increasing returns on investment. Big players in the digital space, such as Amazon, Google, and Meta continue to push for higher bandwidth and greater data processing capabilities, driving a relentless cycle of expansion.

As for the physical layer, although the internet's architecture was theoretically designed to be flexible and scalable down, its financial and institutional underpinnings are firmly tied to a paradigm of endless growth. The financial and governance structures of the internet further reinforce this growth imperative. The financialization of internet infrastructure – fuelled by venture capital, R&D investments, and global competition – mirrors the dynamics of other technological regimes under capitalism, such as fossil fuels and energy grids. Investments in internet-based technologies have skyrocketed, particularly in the United States and China, raising expectations for returns and future sector growth. This finance-driven model has led to the standardization of digital systems worldwide, locking the internet into a growth-dependent trajectory. Climate change and resource scarcity introduce additional challenges. Submarine cable maintenance and data centre refrigeration are already costly, and rising global temperatures, geopolitical conflicts, and microchip shortages will likely compound these issues. These vulnerabilities push companies to justify ever-larger investments and returns, perpetuating a cycle of expansion. As a result, the internet's infrastructure is locked into a path that prioritizes scaling up over exploring smaller, less energy-intensive alternatives. In essence, while the internet was not designed with a deliberate growth agenda, its physical designs, financial models, and global adoption have entrenched it in a paradigm of endless expansion. Rethinking this trajectory is essential to envisioning a more sustainable and equitable digital future.

The present and futures of our infrastructures

Designed for scalability and surrounded by the promise of dematerializing the economy, the internet has become a mega-infrastructure that both drives and is driven by growth. Like other major infrastructures, such as electricity grids, internet expansion is fuelled by technological factors – load factors, backup systems, and over-dimensioned equipment – as well as economic incentives, like maximizing returns on investment and data monetization. However, unlike traditional infrastructures, the internet's logical layer, built from information and protocols, offers more potential for social control and reconfiguration. In a post growth scenario, the internet would likely consume only a fraction of its current energy and material resources, operating under collective governance. Yet, the intricate network of submarine cables, data centres, and power dynamics sustaining the internet's 'stack' makes it challenging to envision how it could meet the necessary reductions in energy and resource use to align with climate goals. To explore this, we can consider several scenarios.

One scenario is collapse, where the immense energy and material flows needed to sustain the stack are no longer available or are redirected towards essential needs, like food production. In this case, the internet as we know it would shrink, with only basic, low-bandwidth connections remaining. This could lead to extreme commodification, where access is restricted to elites. While such a collapse would erode the internet's role in neoliberal globalization, it could also undermine its potential for fostering commons-based peer production, free information sharing, and self-organization – essential tools for degrowth-oriented societies.

A more constructive scenario envisions a 'sober internet'. In this model, the internet would prioritize essential services and applications with clear social and environmental benefits. Collective moral decisions, quotas, and sufficiency policies would ensure equitable access while reversing the trend of ever-expanding internet traffic. Simultaneously, accelerated improvements in data centre energy efficiency would help reduce the environmental impact. Scholars and activists have proposed frameworks that align with degrowth-compatible ideas of the internet, building on contributions from the low-tech movement. Concepts such as slow computing (Kitchin and Fraser, 2020), post-automation (Smith and Fressoli, 2021), and technopolitics and platform cooperativism (Scholz, 2016) emphasize reconfiguring the stack to align with sustainable and democratic principles.

Nevertheless, these efforts face significant challenges. Key questions emerge around how to make submarine cables, data centres, and software systems both sustainable and democratically governed. This demands an extraordinary imaginative effort – not only to conceive of social mechanisms capable of managing complex infrastructures, such as ports, airports, electric grids, and highways democratically, but also to redirect our investments towards new forms of innovation that can make such a transformation possible. Moreover, this line of thinking compels us to confront the possibility that some infrastructures may be fundamentally incompatible with a post growth society and will therefore need to be decommissioned, repurposed, or abandoned. The situation becomes even more complex when we consider how to handle so-called sacrifice zones in a post growth context – places such as nuclear waste sites or heavily contaminated industrial areas. How can we coexist with the ruins of capitalism in a post growth era? How can present infrastructures be reimagined as convivial tools? Moreover, as infrastructures designed for infinite growth inevitably decay, how long should society continue investing in their repair? What are the social and political trade-offs of maintaining or letting go of such systems? Ultimately, rethinking the internet and other key infrastructures for a post growth future requires addressing these difficult questions and balancing the technical, social, and environmental aspects of this complex infrastructure.

The first step towards reimagining infrastructures with a post growth mindset is to recognize that they are often fundamentally designed to enable and reinforce expansion and growth. Further research is urgently needed to identify leverage points for disrupting these entrenched growth dynamics.

Potential interventions could include regulatory reforms, cultural shifts, economic restructuring, or alternatives emerging from social movements, such as open-source initiatives, slow computing, and climate-related activism. To achieve this, we advocate for greater collaboration between the degrowth community and scholars specializing in STS, large technological systems, innovation, and infrastructure. Such interdisciplinary engagement could lead to more nuanced frameworks that uncover the diverse processes and interacting factors driving the rise and decline of infrastructures. The internet provides a compelling case study due to its pervasive role in shaping the lives of billions worldwide. However, similar analyses must extend to other essential mega-infrastructures – such as housing, nuclear plants and their toxic waste, transportation, energy and water supply, the military-industrial complex, and monetary systems. These infrastructures are central to any understanding of prosperity and well-being, yet their significant resource and energy demands make scaling down without compromising quality of life a formidable challenge.

SIX

What Does it Mean Today to Democratize Technology?

We began this book with a reflection on Trump's re-election, which he described as 'a mandate to completely and totally reverse a horrible betrayal and all of these many betrayals that have taken place, and to give the people back their faith, their wealth, their democracy, and, indeed, their freedom'.[1] His supporters see his re-election as a return to democracy, while others view Trump as posing a fundamental threat to democracy. During his second inauguration ceremony, he was accompanied by a grotesque assembly of evangelical pastors, post-truth strategists, and Silicon Valley executives – many of whom transitioned almost instantaneously from backing the Democrats to championing the new Trump era. Beyond the anti-scientific rhetoric, hyper-religious discourse, and xenophobic narratives, what stands out is the almost messianic role attributed to technology embodied in the figure of Elon Musk attending the ceremony. In this farcical scenario, technology is framed as the ultimate solution to America's problems – from reviving stagnant economic growth and fixing inefficient bureaucracy to establishing colonies on Mars. But most importantly for the purposes of this chapter, technology, specifically AI, is being hailed as a means to bypass governmental bureaucracy – which is deemed inefficient and undemocratic. In their attempt to create AI systems that are free from ideological bias, Silicon Valley elites aspire to create tools for replacing politics and democratic decision-making.[2]

Trump's declaration that his new term represents a moment of liberation and the restoration of democracy in America is particularly ironic, given that the word 'democracy' does not even appear in the US Constitution. As David Graeber famously pointed out, the founding fathers of the United States were deeply sceptical of democracy, associating it with unchecked freedom, equality, disorder, and populist uprisings (Graeber, 2007). In this context, the unlikely alliance of radical religious figures and Silicon Valley elites seems to follow a historical pattern – one that resists democracy in its truest form: genuine participation by the people, grounded in equal opportunities and conditions. Elon Musk's recent obsession with applying AI to improve the public administration in the United States is a clear example of this dynamic.[3] By deploying AI in areas where failure is inevitable or at least very probable, these tech elites circumvent democratic debate, creating crises that only they can resolve (McQuillan, 2022). This manufactured dependency ensures that governance remains under corporate influence, further eroding public oversight and control.

This rhetoric surrounding democracy is far from new and extends well beyond the borders of the United States. Democracy has long been heralded as a cornerstone of the so-called Western superiority, often portrayed as the greatest gift of Western tradition to the rest of the world. From a young age, we have been inundated with stories of ancient Athens and its democratic ideals, with vivid images of Athenians gathering at the Areopagus nearly two millennia ago to enact the 'power of the people'. Yet, this narrative often glosses over Athens' reality as a militaristic, xenophobic society that was deeply misogynistic and reliant on slavery. Despite these contradictions, Athens continues to be celebrated as a beacon of good democratic governance. This idealization persists despite ample evidence, as Graeber (2007) has shown, that governance rooted in collective decision-making and equality is not an anomaly in human history but rather a norm, especially in smaller communities. However, even as modern representative democracy in industrialized nations is often recognized as incomplete, flawed, or even inadequate, many in the West regard it as the defining feature that sets us apart from authoritarian or 'uncivilized' societies.

Most of us, having been brought up in liberal democracies, would find it intolerable to live in a country where civil rights are restricted, free speech is suppressed, and press freedom is non-existent. Our media frequently condemns countries like Russia or China for their authoritarian rule and alleged lack of democracy, while being notably less critical of others, such as Saudi Arabia or Qatar. At the same time, most of us regularly accept authoritarian structures in other areas of life. For instance, while we resist being dictated to in our personal lives – how to act, dress, speak, or associate – we often spend a third of our lives in undemocratic, hierarchical organizations: private companies, universities, trade unions, and many others. We are quick to criticize the undemocratic actions of strongmen like Vladimir Putin or Kim Jong Un, yet we rarely question the decision-making processes in our workplaces.

This quiet acceptance of undemocratic practices – defined here as those where people have limited voice and agency in shaping matters that directly affect them – also extends to our relationship with technology and innovation. It's evident, for example, in the consolidation of power by corporate giants like Apple, Google, and Meta, the opacity of their algorithms, pervasive concerns around data ownership and privacy, and the prevalence of top-down 'solutionism' that offers little room for public input. Crucially, innovations and technologies have a direct bearing on our everyday life: they impact our natural environment, our jobs, our mental health, our communities, and our social relations. And yet, individuals are often relegated to passive roles (for example, users, consumers), with limited agency to shape processes of design, funding allocation, governance, and ownership of technologies whose lives, and those of their communities, directly depend on.

Although many companies in Europe are predominantly small and medium-sized enterprises, with the exception of the coops movement that still represents a minority,[4] they are often family-run businesses that lack democratic and egalitarian management principles. The situation is even more pronounced in large corporations that drive global technological advancements. Companies like Apple, Google, Meta, and Microsoft are enormous hierarchical entities, with economic power comparable to that of small nations. Yet, democracy, in any meaningful sense, is almost entirely absent from their structures.

If we redefine democracy as a practical process involving shared responsibility, the ability to listen, empathize, and mediate among peers – and if we accept that technology and society are mutually shaped and constructed as we argued in the previous chapters – it becomes clear that these organizations are ill-suited to develop technologies that truly support democratic principles. This chapter explores theories of democratizing technology and examines recent efforts to steer innovation in new directions, highlighting both their limitations and their potential to transcend the current status quo.

Democratizing technology

The ecological transition presents a paradox. While technological advancements promise efficiency, sustainability, and resource substitution, they also pose the risk of entrenching existing hierarchies and exacerbating social exclusion. The assumption that technological progress is inherently beneficial or neutral masks the ways in which it often privileges certain groups while further marginalizing others. In this context, as we argued several times in this book, democratizing technology becomes not just a technical issue but a deeply political one, requiring a fundamental reconfiguration of how decisions about innovation and technological implementation are made.

DEMOCRATIZING TECHNOLOGY

It is indisputable that historically technological choices have been shaped by elite interests, reinforcing centralized control and limiting opportunities for democratic engagement. Even when technology was deliberately designed to promote horizontal self-management and organization, like in the case of the internet, the forces of capitalism have slowly co-opted and reconfigured it the serve the interests of a small number of big actors. So why has democracy not been extended to technically mediated domains of social life, despite centuries of political struggle? According to Andrew Feenberg (2001), it is not because technology is inherently undemocratic but because it has been systematically used to block democratic participation. Corporate and military leaders, professional associations, and engineers exert more influence over technological development than elected governments. As a result, technology often serves corporate and bureaucratic interests rather than collective social needs. One manifestation of this dynamic is the increasing complexity of modern technologies. The shift to electric cars, for instance, exemplifies how technological systems can enhance safety while simultaneously reducing user control. As we discussed in Chapter 3, greater dependence on proprietary software and manufacturer maintenance means that end-users have limited capacity to repair or modify their vehicles. This complexity creates new layers of exclusion, making it difficult for ordinary users to challenge or understand the decisions embedded within technological systems. Similarly, digital platforms, while ostensibly fostering connectivity and efficiency, often reinforce monopolistic control and diminish democratic oversight.

The ideology of technological determinism discussed in Chapter 2 – presented through notions of efficiency, productivity, and necessity – serves as a justification for restricting democratic participation. This deterministic outlook falsely suggests that certain technological trajectories and choices are inevitable and must be embraced without question. However, this view is not only flawed but dangerous, as it removes the possibility of critical thinking and collective decision-making from the process of technological change. An alternative perspective is needed – one that goes beyond technocratic governance and instead fosters radical democratic engagement with technology. Feenberg's (2001) concept of subversive rationalization argues for reclaiming technology as a source of public power rather than corporate control. This requires participatory design processes that actively involve workers, users, and marginalized communities in decision-making. Rather than allowing technological systems to be dictated by elite interests, these communities must be empowered to shape technological outcomes according to their own needs and values.

Resistance to undemocratic technological systems has historically emerged from diverse sources, including labour struggles, environmental movements, and opposition to nuclear energy. These forms of resistance highlight the necessity of incorporating externalities – such as environmental and social consequences – into technological decision-making, and they are also a call for a more direct involvement of people into the process. Beyond resistance, democratization requires both technical and political transformation. Feenberg (1992) argues that if authoritarian social hierarchies are not an inherent necessity of technological progress, then alternative models of rationalization must be explored. This challenges deterministic views of modern technology as incompatible with democracy. While neoliberalism has used technology to expand bureaucratic control – exemplified by the increasing managerialism in universities and IT-driven workplace surveillance – these same technologies could, in a different social context, be repurposed to support democratic governance and collective decision-making. The work of Graeber and Wengrow (2021) in this sense opens up historical possibilities for non-hierarchical forms of managing complex technological systems. Many traditional societies have developed sophisticated governance structures without resorting to rigid hierarchies. The assumption that modernity necessitates centralized control must therefore be questioned. There is no single path to technological development; instead, multiple possibilities exist, each shaped by different social choices.

In the previous chapters we problematized the positions of part of post growth/degrowth communities that see technology either as neutral tools that can be replaced with inherently non-growth-driven artefacts or as inevitably bad and destructive. We think that democratizing technology means rejecting the binary opposition between rational technological progress and an irrational return to nature. Thinkers like Weber, Ellul, and Heidegger have portrayed technology as an inescapable force that enslaves humanity, leaving no hope for democratic intervention. However, this fatalistic perspective must be also challenged. Technology is neither inherently oppressive nor inherently liberatory. Its impact depends on the social structures that drive its development and adoption and within which it is embedded. The way forward involves rethinking innovation beyond market-driven imperatives and towards collective well-being. This means not just creating new technologies but actively withdrawing from harmful technological trajectories, as suggested by Goulet and Vinck (2023) in their discussions of the new horizons for innovation studies. Whether in sectors such as agriculture, digital infrastructure, or industrial production, the structuring principle of future innovations should not be the relentless introduction of novelties but the deliberate removal of exploitative systems. Extending democracy into the realm of technology is not a utopian aspiration but a necessity. It requires dismantling the ideological barriers that portray technological change as a neutral or inevitable process. By actively engaging diverse social groups in shaping technological futures, societies can move towards a model where innovation serves collective interests rather than reinforcing elite control. Only through such radical reimagining can technology become a true instrument of democracy rather than a tool of exclusion and domination.

The empty rhetoric of mission-oriented innovation

There is growing awareness about the need to put science and technology at the service of people. In particular, the European Union has made efforts to develop frameworks for innovation that incorporate principles of ethics, responsibility, and liability. Concepts such as Ethical, Social, and Legal Assessment and Technology Assessment have been promoted in both Europe and the United States as mechanisms to ensure that technological advancements align with societal needs. More recently, the notion of mission-oriented innovation has gained traction as a way to steer technological development towards addressing large-scale social and environmental challenges. Proponents such as Mazzucato and Perez (2023) advocate for a redirection of economic and technological growth towards sustainable and inclusive ends. However, this perspective fails to engage with the fundamental issue underlying technological production: the deeply entrenched undemocratic structures of capitalism.

The OECD (2021) asserts that 'mission-oriented innovation policies, governance, and practices support directed action toward achieving ambitious goals'. But the question remains: who determines these goals? The methodologies proposed for stakeholder engagement remain top-down, structured in ways that do not democratize decision-making in the very places where technological innovation is produced. Companies, which are hierarchical and profit-driven by nature, continue to dictate the trajectory of technological development, largely insulated from democratic influence. Even frameworks like Responsible Research and Innovation attempt to introduce public engagement mechanisms but fail to democratize the core processes of technological production. Without addressing the undemocratic structures of corporate power, mission-oriented innovation remains an empty slogan, incapable of fostering genuine societal transformation.

At its core, mission-oriented innovation remains locked within a paradigm of economic growth. Advocates argue for a different kind of growth – one that is sustainable, green – but they seldom question the necessity of growth itself. This is where their vision falls short. While conventional innovation policy has already demonstrated its failures (Uyarra et al, 2019), proposals for transformative innovation (Schot and Steinmueller, 2018) still assume that the solution lies in directing growth rather than fundamentally rethinking it. The assumption that economic expansion can be guided towards social good overlooks the reality that growth has always been directed – historically, by imperialism and, in the present, by corporate elites. The goal is never truly democratization but a rebranding of state intervention within the capitalist framework.

Moreover, the vision of green growth is fundamentally flawed. Green technologies, often touted as the key to sustainability, are themselves products of the same economic forces that fuelled environmental destruction in the first place. The belief that smarter, more efficient government policies can steer growth towards sustainable outcomes ignores the fact that the root problem lies in the economic imperative to maximize efficiency and profit. A genuine shift away from this paradigm would require not merely redirecting growth but abandoning its logic entirely. This would entail reducing economic activities, shortening working hours, and collectively deciding what and how to produce in a democratic manner – long before investing in technological advancement under the guise of sustainability.

The failure of mission-oriented innovation to address democracy is evident in the policy briefs of its key proponents. For instance, Hekkert et al (2020) do not even mention democracy in their discussions of mission-oriented innovation systems. Similarly, Borrás and Edler (2020) discuss the role of the state in innovation but fail to acknowledge that the state itself is deeply intertwined with capitalist logic. The state does not function as a neutral actor capable of steering innovation towards social good; rather, it is an institution that works symbiotically with private capital. This oversight is especially troubling coming from scholars rooted in evolutionary economics and post-Keynesian thought, who should recognize that capitalism's structural constraints cannot be overcome through better policy alone.

Ultimately, mission-oriented innovation serves as another rhetorical repackaging of existing economic structures rather than a true break from them. While it emphasizes stakeholder engagement, it fails to address how democratic agency is exercised within technology production. The reluctance to embrace the necessity of economic planning further reveals its ideological limitations. In a neoliberal landscape where planning is taboo – dismissed as reminiscent of Soviet centralization – advocates of mission-oriented innovation shy away from acknowledging that real democracy in technological development would require a radical restructuring of economic power (Devine, 1989). Going beyond growth does not mean replacing bad growth with good growth or inefficient economies with efficient ones. It requires a fundamental departure from the economic logic that prioritizes profit and efficiency above all else. The Japanese translation of 'degrowth' by Nakano Yoshihiro (2010) captures this shift through three kanji: 脱 'Exit', 成長 'growth', or simply 'farewell to growth' (Datsu-Seichou in Japanese). This is not merely a change in technological priorities; it is an epistemological and ontological transformation that challenges the economic order itself.

Mazzucato and Perez, despite their criticisms of free-market fundamentalism, ultimately fail to grasp – or intentionally ignore – that capitalism structurally dictates the course of innovation. Intentions are irrelevant within a system designed to prioritize corporate profit. As Joel Bakan (2004) demonstrated in *The Corporation*, corporations behave as legal persons but exhibit sociopathic tendencies: they act without conscience, prioritize profit over ethical considerations, and continue harmful practices regardless of leadership changes. The corporate imperative to maximize shareholder value ensures that any attempt to 'steer' innovation remains subject to the same capitalist pressures that have historically driven environmental destruction, labour exploitation, and social inequality. If we are to take democracy and technology seriously, we must go beyond mission-oriented innovation and confront the reality that technological progress under capitalism is inherently undemocratic. This means expanding democracy into the realm of production itself, dismantling corporate hierarchies, and fundamentally reimagining economic organization. Anything less is merely an exercise in empty rhetoric, offering the illusion of change while preserving the structures that prevent true democratic participation in technological development.

What we can learn from failed experiments

As we have previously discussed, technology has long been a site of contestation and resistance. From the Luddites to factory occupations in Argentina, there is a deep tradition of reclaiming democratic control over technology and production (Smith, 2005). In this section, we examine a few experiments that illuminate these dynamics. These cases are just examples that we selected to show their potential to trigger new imaginaries about how the relation between work and production of new technology can be articulated on the premises of radical democracy.

The Lucas Plan remains one of the most significant examples of radical technological democracy in recent history. Emerging in the mid-1970s, it was initiated by workers at Lucas Aerospace, a major British manufacturer of military and aerospace components, who faced the threat of layoffs and plant closures. Instead of passively accepting their fate, they organized under the Lucas Aerospace Combine Shop Stewards' Committee and proposed an alternative vision. Their plan sought to pivot the company away from weapons production towards socially useful goods, such as renewable energy technologies, medical devices, and sustainable transportation systems.[5] The plan included around 200 technologies with their associated financial plans. Most of the technologies proposed in the plan had innovative designed and were the result of a collective process based on the interaction with local territories. What made the Lucas Plan groundbreaking was not just its alternative industrial vision but the democratic process behind it (Cooley, 2020). The workers rejected top-down decision-making in favour of a model that emphasized grassroots knowledge in shaping technological development. They experimented with socially useful production – technologies that enhance human autonomy and serve the public good rather than perpetuating profit-driven or centralized control. In this way, the Lucas Plan was an attempt to liberate technology from capitalist constraints and reorient it towards fulfilling human and ecological needs. Through a participatory process, the workers sought to redesign their company's technological priorities, leveraging their hands-on expertise. This approach stood in stark contrast to the technocratic structures that dominate industrial production, where efficiency and profit maximization are often prioritized over social and environmental concerns. Despite its radical vision, the Lucas Plan ultimately failed due to a lack of institutional support and government endorsement. Management rejected the proposal, and unions – deeply entangled in corporatist structures – did not provide the necessary backing. However, its legacy persists as an inspiration for contemporary efforts to envision alternatives to profit-driven technological systems. Its emphasis on socially useful production and worker participation remains a model for rethinking industrial activity in ways that prioritize human well-being and ecological sustainability. In the words of Lucas activist Mike Cooley (2020b: 106) '[the plan] demonstrated beyond any doubt the ability of so-called ordinary workers to decide what products they should make, how they should make them and in whose interests, they should be made'. The legacy of the Lucas Plan remains strong in the UK. A recent report, 'A Lucas Plan for the Twenty-First Century: From Asset Manager

Arsenal to Green Industrial Strategy', published by Common Wealth,[6] examined the technical and financial feasibility of repurposing the British military industry for green technology production (Rogaly, 2024). As part of the study, 21 workers and trade unionists were interviewed. Nearly all expressed openness to expanding their sites into green production, viewing it as technologically feasible. However, their visions for this transition varied – some supported partial diversification alongside military production, while others advocated for a more comprehensive industrial conversion.

Outside the UK as well, the struggle for democratic control over production has manifested in various worker-led initiatives, often emerging in response to economic crises and factory closures. One such example is the Megaride cooperative in Naples, Italy (Pighetti et al, 2009). Founded in the early 2000s, Megaride was born when workers faced the shutdown of a shipyard. Rather than accepting unemployment, they occupied the factory under the slogan 'We'll resist a minute more than the factory owner', also the title of the documentary *Un Minuto in Più*.[7] The occupation lasted for years, with workers spending Christmas Eve in the shipyard alongside their families. Despite their resilience, they were criminalized, sued multiple times for blocking roads in Naples, and some even faced penal court judgments. They also actively participated in local social movements, joining students and other groups fighting for employment rights. However, traditional labour unions offered no support, instead advising them to accept a redundancy plan that would have fired 80 per cent of the workforce, with vague promises of potential rehiring in the future. Despite these obstacles, the workers successfully established a cooperative, securing both public and private contracts. Megaride operated in shipbuilding, serving various sectors, including fishing, naval operations, and ferry transport. Unlike conventional enterprises driven by profit maximization, Megaride prioritized democratic decision-making, fair wages, and job security. Their commitment to a cooperative model challenged dominant market logic, demonstrating that alternative economic structures could thrive even in competitive industries. The workers' skills were widely recognized and valued across Italy. A particularly notable aspect of the Megaride experiment was the period of self-management, during which workers collectively made decisions not only about the organization of labour in the shipyard but also about technical aspects of ship design. This level of autonomy set them apart from traditional workplaces. However, the cooperative faced persistent hostility. Many companies operating in the Naples port sought to reclaim the occupied space, using institutional pressure to undermine Megaride's activities. In 2019, authorities shut down the factory under the pretext of handling hazardous iron materials, effectively putting an end to the cooperative's independent operations. Ultimately, Megaride found itself increasingly isolated, unable to develop strong synergies and connections with similar initiatives locally and nationally. The economic crisis, combined with shifting production trends in Europe that favoured northern regions, and the impact of the COVID-19 pandemic, forced the cooperative to merge with a more powerful, privately owned local company. Today, Megaride remains a cooperative in name, but it has lost the spirit of self-management that defined its struggle from the start. While the workers are still formally part of a cooperative, their work is now structured like that of conventional employees – making them little different from waged workers in a traditional company.

Megaride's experience is not an isolated case. Italy has approximately 400 recuperated enterprises,[8] where workers reclaim abandoned businesses and turn them into cooperatives (Mastrandrea, 2015). One prominent example is RiMaflow,[9] an occupied and self-managed factory in Milan. Originally an auto parts manufacturer under Maflow, the factory closed in 2010, leaving its workers unemployed. In 2013, former employees occupied the site, converting it into a worker-run cooperative focused on recycling, coworking, and sustainable production. Despite its commitment to ecological and social goals, RiMaflow faced legal challenges, with authorities accusing it of handling stolen goods. Police raids and legal troubles highlighted the precarious nature of worker self-management within the constraints of existing economic and legal frameworks. The cooperative remains in an experimental phase, striving to establish itself as a hub for recycling technological devices and machinery.

The ex-GKN factory in Florence represents another significant case of worker-led resistance and industrial transformation. Similar to the case of Lucas, when the British automotive company GKN decided to close the factory in 2021, the workers occupied the site and declared a permanent assembly. With the support of experts and academics from across Italy, they developed an alternative plan to produce photovoltaic panels and electric cargo-bikes (Leonardi and Gabbriellini, 2023). Their struggle is ongoing and uncertain, but to sustain their initiative, they launched a crowdfunding campaign. A key part of this effort is the introduction of a 'solidarity stake' worth one million euros, inviting citizens, associations, movements, trade union delegates, and activists to invest and participate in the cooperative's assembly. This innovative model of 'popular shareholding' allows the people of Florence, alongside international climate and social movements, renewable energy communities, and various associations, to take part in overseeing the reindustrialization process.

The lessons from the Lucas Plan and Megaride, and more generally the recent cases of recuperated factories in Europe, underscore a critical issue: democratic control over production is a necessary but insufficient condition for broader systemic change. Even within worker-controlled enterprises, there is no guarantee that democratic governance will align with broader social and ecological imperatives, such as combatting climate change or fostering international worker solidarity. Moreover, the broader labour movement has often been reluctant to embrace such experiments. Traditional unions, constrained by conventional economic thinking, frequently oppose or neglect worker-led cooperatives, failing to envision alternative modes of resistance (Jossa, 2018). Yet, these experiments reveal an essential truth: without democratizing production, the possibility of a just and sustainable technological transition remains unattainable. The challenge moving forward is not simply to replicate these models but to develop strategies that integrate them into wider networks of mutual support, institutional backing, and post growth economic thinking. As Mike Cooley (2020), said: '[…] there can be no islands of social responsibility in a sea of depravity'. This calls for the rise of a broader social movement capable of integrating not only traditional environmental struggles but also innovative approaches to organizing production. The collapse of the traditional left, coupled with the uncritical embrace of neoliberalism by former communist and socialist parties in the EU, has created a profound intellectual void that demands urgent reimagining. To bridge this gap, a compelling vision must emerge – one that unites the environmental and social imperatives of the degrowth movement with a bold new framework for radical technological democracy.

Towards a post growth science, technology, and innovation policy

Calls to democratize technology have long been present within degrowth traditions. Thinkers like André Gorz and Ivan Illich sought to counter the over-pessimistic perspectives of Jacques Ellul and Martin Heidegger by developing structured imaginaries of socially controlled technological development. This vision of technology placed power in the hands of communities rather than corporations, emphasizing the importance of democratic governance over innovation and production. Recent proposals from degrowth and post growth scholarship have built upon these foundations, offering concrete policy measures that move beyond theoretical critique.

Fitzpatrick et al (2022) documented approximately 530 policy proposals in the degrowth literature, many of which advocate for social control of technology, workplace democracy, and moratoria on controversial technological advancements, such as nuclear power, GMOs, and geo-engineering. Among these, a recurring agenda is the transition towards democratic, not-for-profit business models, including cooperatives, self-production initiatives, small-scale enterprises, and commons-based peer production. These models emphasize relocalization, aiming to cut greenhouse gas emissions while fostering local resilience and autonomy. A central element in the degrowth approach to technology is the concept of technological sovereignty, which proposes halting potentially dangerous industrial-scale interventions, such as geo-engineering and biogenetics. Key measures include regular citizen-led audits on the desirability of new technologies, the restructuring of social media into public or commons-based platforms, the repurposing of military facilities for sustainable production, and the dismantling of patent monopolies – especially in essential areas like seeds and pharmaceuticals. Another pillar of degrowth technology policy is the promotion of convivial tools, ensuring that people can repair and repurpose their tools rather than depend on corporate-controlled infrastructures. This includes initiatives like cooperative repair workshops, local currency systems, and community-supported agriculture. Despite these proposals, much of the existing degrowth literature remains focused on low-tech, localized solutions without sufficient elaboration on large-scale systemic transformations. Furthermore, while degrowth theorists have outlined broad alternatives, the absence of detailed implementation strategies raises concerns about their feasibility in the face of entrenched corporate power and state interests.

Technology is also a key focus of emerging degrowth strategic thinking. Moving from abstract critique to actionable planning, scholars have recognized the necessity of addressing the undemocratic nature of labour under capitalism. Barlow et al (2022) acknowledge that the lack of societal control over technological development is rooted in the capitalist separation of labour from democratic decision-making. They argue that true transformation requires restructuring the relationship between work, technology, and democracy. Yet, despite this recognition, their solutions still largely revolve around an undefined vision of 'low-tech infrastructure', with limited engagement with research on technological systems and governance. One of the most recent contributions, *The Future is Degrowth* by Vetter et al (2023), categorizes potential strategies into interstitial strategies, non-reformist reforms, and efforts to build counter-hegemonic institutions. This includes the creation of 'really-existing' alternative institutions, such as cooperatives and community-based organizations – what they term 'now-topias'. These institutions provide practical, on-the-ground examples of how democratic alternatives to capitalist technological development can function. However, their scalability and integration into broader systemic change remain open questions.

A recent article by Kallis et al (2025), published in *The Lancet*, presents a comprehensive overview of post growth thinking and policy measures, including universal basic income, working-time reduction, universal basic services, job guarantees, maximum income limits, wealth taxes, public monetary reforms, alternative economic indicators to GDP, the Green New Deal, and carbon taxation. However, despite its breadth, the article notably omits proposals *for democratizing science and technological production*. This gap underscores a recurring issue in post growth discourse: while economic and social policies are well-theorized, the role of technological systems and their governance remains an underdeveloped frontier.

In this book we proposed to advance post growth thinking by engaging more explicitly with STS, which could provide valuable insights into the structural and institutional barriers that shape technological development under capitalism. A coherent post growth technology policy must go beyond simply reducing high-tech dependency or promoting local alternatives. It must grapple with the political economy of technological development, recognizing that the trajectory of innovation is not neutral but shaped by capitalist imperatives, even apparently post growth compatible artefacts like bicycles. We began in Chapters 1 and 2 by deconstructing the discourse of innovation as deterministic and neutral. We aimed to show that technologies are not merely artefacts or tools but rather systems comprising interconnected technologies, social structures, and power relations. This has profound implications for post growth planning, as it calls for the development of a broad political and technological programme capable of reversing and dismantling the growth-driven mechanisms embedded in modern societies.

In Chapter 3, we proposed an alternative way to frame technology – one grounded in the notion of care. This approach seeks to balance our obsession with 'the new', embodied in the concept of innovation, with the practice of caring, as exemplified by the diverse R2R movement. Chapter 4 extended these ideas to organizations. We first identified specific features that emerge from the analysis of alternative organizational forms. We then argued that a post growth organization must necessarily be rooted in radical democracy. A genuine democratization of technology requires direct engagement with production processes, ensuring that technological choices prioritize collective well-being over profit. This involves not only supporting alternative models, such as worker cooperatives and commons-based production, but also actively resisting the monopolization of knowledge and innovation by private interests. Without addressing these structural issues, post growth technological policy risks remaining a collection of scattered initiatives rather than a transformative force capable of reshaping the future of science and innovation. The challenge is not just to envision a different technological paradigm but to build the political and institutional frameworks necessary to make it a reality.

Finally, in Chapter 5, we extended our analysis to infrastructure, emphasizing the importance of recognizing the materiality of the technological systems that underpin modern life. These infrastructures are often designed according to assumptions of perpetual growth. We argued for their democratization, as well as for the urgent need to envision strategies for the decommissioning of infrastructures that are incompatible with a post growth society – such as nuclear power plants and fossil fuel facilities.

We think that a necessary step towards advancing these ideas is the construction of a collective subject capable of embracing and implementing them. This requires engaging not only counter-hegemonic social movements but also traditional political actors, such as unions and progressive parties, that remain trapped in productivist or eco-modernist visions of technology and sustainability. As we showed in Chapter 3, for the R2R, the emergence of this new political subject might be based on the convergence of various struggles, including demands for more responsible innovation and social control over technology, hackers, citizen science and fab labs movements, climate activism, and movements defending rural areas from depopulation. These efforts should work in tandem with grassroots environmental movements resisting large-scale infrastructure projects, such as wind farms, dams, nuclear plants, and other megaprojects associated with ecological and social harm. Such alliances may also necessitate strategic cooperation with political actors who, while not fully aligned with degrowth or eco-socialist perspectives, share the goal of reclaiming democratic control over technology. However, embracing these changes does not imply a simplistic return to an idealized low-tech past. It is not about rejecting complexity outright but rather about designing technological systems that operate within planetary boundaries. Achieving sustainability will require reducing overconsumption to levels compatible with ecological limits, but this does not mean abandoning innovation or regressing to pre-industrial lifestyles. Instead, the challenge is to redefine what progress means and to orient technological development towards sufficiency, autonomy, and collective well-being rather than perpetual expansion.

The political subject capable of spearheading these transformations remains an open question. To conclude this chapter, we propose two hypotheses that future research must address. First, sustaining science, technology, and innovation systems within a non-growing economy will necessitate a radical restructuring of scientific, financial, and political institutions. This transformation must involve new funding mechanisms and incentives that foster reflexive, democratic, and inclusive innovation processes. Additionally, it calls for alternative indicators and benchmarks for measuring success beyond economic growth.

Second, an unexplored but crucial area of study concerns the variety of organizational forms that engage in innovation without being driven by expansionist imperatives. The cases examined in this and previous chapters suggest that organizations grounded in horizontal and democratic governance structures – such as cooperatives, community-led initiatives, and commons-based institutions – are more likely to cultivate innovation that aligns with degrowth principles. These organizations not only create technological artefacts but also foster new social arrangements and institutional models that minimize ecological impact while enhancing autonomy and conviviality. By doing so, they provide valuable insights into the power structures and organizational configurations necessary to move towards a new paradigm of innovation untethered from economic growth.

Building on these working hypotheses, we suggest a research agenda aimed at deepening the study of post growth organizational models. A first priority is to develop a coherent theoretical framework that synthesizes diverse academic traditions – degrowth studies, ecological economics, critical theory, and critical management studies – into a unified vision of science, technology, and innovation systems liberated from the imperatives of capitalist growth. To date, these fields have remained fragmented, and their potential to inform a transformative technological politics remains underexplored.

A second research priority is to identify the conditions under which non-growth-oriented technological systems can emerge and flourish. Existing scholarship has only begun to address this issue, with management studies making tentative inquiries into post growth organizational settings, while degrowth scholars have only recently started focusing on these topics. More empirical research is needed to understand how such organizations self-organize, navigate financial and logistical constraints, and resist pressures to conform to conventional growth paradigms.

Another crucial area of investigation concerns alternative supply chains and production networks. Most research on non-growth-oriented economies has been confined to the study of alternative food networks, but the same questions must be asked of other critical infrastructures, including energy, transportation, and digital services. Understanding how post growth organizations can integrate into, challenge, or transform existing economic systems is essential for creating viable pathways towards systemic change. These inquiries should also explore hybrid approaches to infrastructure management.[10] Experiments with cooperative ownership of essential services, such as internet networks, water distribution, and energy grids, suggest that communal control is feasible. However, integrating these models into existing infrastructures – many of which remain under private ownership – raises complex questions about governance, regulation, and economic sustainability. Future research must address these challenges and develop strategies for transitioning towards democratically managed infrastructures that function outside the logic of economic expansion.

Finally, no transformative shift can succeed without political mobilization. Future research must identify the social actors and institutions most capable of triggering a transition to post growth innovation. This requires analysing how alliances between different social movements, political struggles, and institutional reforms can be built. Theories of social movements as agents of change, as well as studies on the institutionalization and deinstitutionalization of economic paradigms, offer valuable insights into how degrowth-oriented technological governance might gain traction. Ultimately, rethinking the future of technology in a post growth world requires moving beyond critique and articulating viable alternatives. This means engaging in both theoretical reflection and practical experimentation, drawing lessons from existing initiatives while identifying pathways for broader systemic transformation. The challenge ahead is not just to imagine a different technological paradigm but to create the political and institutional conditions that will make it possible.

Coda: Why Did We Stop Making Experiments?

In *The Utopia of Rules: On Technology, Stupidity, and the Secret Joys of Bureaucracy*, David Graeber (2015) writes: 'The ultimate, hidden truth of the world is that it is something that we make, and could just as easily make differently'. The paradox of our contemporary obsession with innovation is that while it is often celebrated as a tribute to creativity, it frequently functions as an intellectual cage – one in which only certain ideas are permitted to flourish, while broader imagination is stifled and constrained. Living in that cage makes it difficult to imagine how things could be done differently. We began this book with Mark Fisher's concept of capitalist realism – the pervasive notion that it is impossible to imagine, let alone desire, a world beyond growth-driven capitalism. This mental trap echoes technological determinism, productivism, and the illusion of control over our actions, all of which reinforce the belief that there is only one possible way to organize society. Yet, we find ourselves disoriented amidst the overwhelming complexities derived from multiple crises – environmental, social, and psychological – all of which demand a break from this imposed inevitability. Both capitalist realism and technological determinism impose a horizon of possibilities that we do need to question. Horizons, as culturally ingrained assumptions, shape our understanding of technology and social organization, yet history shows that they are neither universal nor immutable.

In other words, despite being praised as a system that encourages creativity and free enterprise, capitalism is a social system that destroys, or in the best case, limits imagination, appropriates creativity, and suppresses social experimentation.

CODA

Even our most advanced technology, AI, no matter how creative it may seem, is still trained on abstractions drawn from the past. As a result, it tends to rearrange existing ideas rather than truly reimagine how the world could or should be (McQuillan, 2022). Feenberg critiques technological determinism and productivism, which he encapsulated under the term 'rationalization' – the instrumental approach to science, technology, and innovation that prioritizes optimization, efficiency, and endless growth. This rationalization serves capital and entrenches a form of technological development that subordinates human and ecological concerns to profit. But rationalization, much like past justifications for child labour or exploitative industrial practices, is a historical construct rather than an immutable law. Technological rationality is not universal but rather a product of capitalism. In a society organized around worker cooperatives, a different rationality would emerge – one focused on democratically controlled productivity rather than corporate-led productivism. Yet, this does not guarantee an automatic transition to a post growth society. A new rationality might merely shift control from corporate boards to workers' councils without fundamentally altering the drive for expansion. However, opening the door to a plurality of technological governance models marks a crucial step towards democratizing innovation. Feenberg, and Marcuse before him, advance Marxist analysis by arguing that the problem is not merely ownership – whether capitalist or socialist – but the broader power structures that mediate sociotechnical relations. The distinction lies between societies where technical mediation concentrates power and those where it is democratized.

As we showed in Chapter 2, technology's social meaning and functional rationality are inextricably linked. As soon as technical codes become standardized, they appear naturalized, masking the social forces behind them. But the fundamental choices that societies make about technology – whether to prioritize climate destruction or sustainable and pro-worker innovation – are not simply trade-offs in economic efficiency. They are ethical decisions about whether human and ecological well-being should come before profit. Collegial forms of technical control, like guilds and cooperatives, are not inherently incompatible with technological advancement – only with capitalism's logic of accumulation. Capitalist realism obscures the fundamental fabric of human society, which David Graeber called 'playground communism' – our innate ability to cooperate, share, and self-organize. Technological determinism reinforces the illusion that technology is beyond social control, dismissing any attempt at intervention as authoritarian. Graeber's work highlights the persistent space for creativity and imagination in shaping technology, which in turn challenges the dogma of technological inevitability.

Democratizing production at multiple levels – beyond the local and beyond simplistic 'low-tech' solutions – is the first step in separating innovation from the drive for growth. Innovation will still be necessary, but what will it mean once detached from the imperative of expansion? The Brazilian composer Antônio Carlos Jobim composed a sweet bossa nova melody using only one note (Samba de uma Nota Só), proving that creativity thrives under constraints. Similarly, we must rethink technological creativity – not merely in the endless pursuit of novelty but in fostering maintenance, care, and repair. Creativity can manifest in withdrawal, in slowing down, in doing with less. In addition, mainstream innovation theories recognize that regulation and bans can themselves become sources of creativity. Banning single-use plastics or toxic chemicals forces industries to rethink their processes. Slowing down technological cycles, as suggested by Kitchin and Fraser (2020) and Goulet and Vinck (2023), could open new avenues for post growth innovation. Innovation need not always mean adoption; it can mean de-adoption. It can mean resisting the drive to constantly introduce new technologies, instead prioritizing durability, repurposing, and communal access. The CoopCycle initiative, examined in Chapter 4, demonstrates that technology can diverge from its original corporate logic and be reshaped by user communities. The socio-political context in which technologies are designed and used determines their trajectory. The challenge lies not in eliminating technology but in ensuring that its governance aligns with social and ecological needs.

The key question is not whether a post growth society means abandoning washing machines or other modern conveniences but how such technologies can be produced democratically and sustainably. Must washing machines remain the domain of global corporate monopolies, or can we imagine local production networks inspired by the Lucas Plan – where manufacturing reflects local needs while maintaining global cooperation? These questions should not be dismissed as unrealistic but explored as alternatives to the false dichotomy of nationalization versus offshoring. In Europe, countless factories are closed under the guise of inefficiency and unprofitability. Instead of relying on state nationalization, which often perpetuates existing power structures, we should advocate for democratizing production itself. Simply transferring ownership from private corporations to the state does not guarantee democratic control or ecological sustainability. Nationalization, while a common response to privatization's failures, does not automatically dismantle the underlying logic of growth-driven production. A more transformative approach is required – one that prioritizes participatory decision-making, technological sovereignty, and reorienting production towards social needs rather than profit. The challenge is to envision economic structures beyond traditional state ownership models – ones that are socially just and ecologically viable.

The transition to post growth will be messy, incomplete, and hybrid. While strong social movements can push governments to act, the process will never be linear. Various configurations of relationships between states, people, and cooperatives will emerge. Echoing David Graeber's final works, we must ask why affluent Western societies have abandoned the experimentation with alternative organizational models that once flourished. The self-management system in Yugoslavia, for example, exemplified a large-scale experiment in decentralizing decision-making (Santo, 2024). During Tito's leadership, Yugoslav factories operated under a model of worker self-management, where employees collectively decided on production, investment, and distribution. This experiment, while imperfect, demonstrated that economic democracy is possible at scale. The interconnected principles of autonomy, commons-based governance, and universal basic services remain integral to degrowth and post growth visions. The Yugoslav model offers valuable lessons in economic democratization, illustrating how power can be decentralized from elites to workers and citizens. Similarly, experiments in 1970s Western Europe sought to redefine industrial organization outside the capitalist growth imperative. We conclude by advocating for systematic research into institutional experimentation as a critical step towards democratizing technological innovation. Post growth societies will require new governance structures, new alliances, and new ways of imagining technological futures. Social change occurs when ordinary people come together and declare that the status quo is untenable. This is how societies have historically transformed, and it is how they can do so again.

Notes

Introduction: What Do You Believe? A Miracle of Technology or Politics?

1. There is an ongoing debate about the distinction between post growth and degrowth. In our view, degrowth is rooted in a specific activist and academic tradition, tracing back to the ideas of André Gorz in the 1970s and Serge Latouche in the 1990s. Post growth, on the other hand, is a broader concept that includes degrowth alongside other perspectives, such as doughnut economics, well-being economics, steady-state economics, and political ecology. In this book, we argue that while so-called rich countries will inevitably need to degrow, the longer-term goal should be to cultivate a post growth vision – one that moves beyond an economic system centred on perpetual growth.

2. Eco-modernism is an environmental philosophy that sees technological progress and human development as essential tools for achieving ecological sustainability. Unlike traditional environmentalism, which often emphasizes limits to growth, eco-modernism argues that innovation can help reduce humanity's impact on the planet while still improving living standards. It promotes the idea of 'decoupling', where economic and social progress become less dependent on natural resource consumption through advancements such as clean energy, high-yield farming, and industrial efficiency. Urbanization is also seen as a key factor in protecting nature, as dense, well-planned cities reduce land use and environmental damage. Eco-modernists are generally optimistic about human ingenuity, believing that science and technology can solve environmental challenges rather than requiring radical societal shifts or degrowth. They argue that economic growth and environmental protection can coexist, provided that policies and innovations guide development in a sustainable direction. See the Ecomodernist Manifesto available here: https://www.ecomodernism.org/

3. In *The Imaginary Institution of Society*, Cornelius Castoriadis (1998) argues that society is not merely a product of rational structures or economic forces but is fundamentally shaped by the collective imagination. He challenges structuralist and Marxist views by emphasizing that institutions, meanings, and norms are not predetermined but are created through an ongoing social-historical process. Central to his argument is the concept of the radical imaginary, which refers to society's ability to create new forms, values, and institutions beyond existing frameworks.

This imaginary dimension is what enables genuine social change and autonomy, as opposed to mere reproduction of established structures. Thus, Castoriadis redefines social institutions as not just functional entities but as deeply rooted in the creative and symbolic capacities of human societies. In this sense, the idea of progress or endless economic growth can be seen as a form of radical imaginaries. But as Kallis (2019) shows in his book *Limits*, society can be also organized around self-imposed limits.

[4] The EU parliament organized two 'Beyond Growth' conferences. More info at: https://www.beyond-growth-2023.eu/

one   The Growth Delusion: How Innovation Fuels Our Path to Disaster

[1] The Prime Minister said: 'Congratulations president-elect Trump on your historic election victory. I look forward to working with you in the years ahead. As the closest of allies, we stand shoulder to shoulder in defence of our shared values of freedom, democracy and enterprise. From growth and security to innovation and tech, I know that the UK-US special relationship will continue to prosper on both sides of the Atlantic for years to come'. Source: https://www.independent.co.uk/news/uk/donald-trump-keir-starmer-david-lammy-ukraine-white-house-b2642281.html

[2] Backstop technology, a concept introduced by economist William Nordhaus, refers to a hypothetical, unlimited, and cost-effective alternative energy source that becomes available when fossil fuel prices rise significantly. It serves as a long-term safety net, preventing resource depletion from causing extreme economic disruptions. The idea is central to Nordhaus's economic models on climate change and energy, suggesting that technological progress will eventually provide sustainable solutions to fossil fuel dependency.

[3] The Nobel Memorial Prize in Economic Sciences is not one of the original Nobel Prizes established by Alfred Nobel's will in 1895. It was created in 1968 by the Swedish Central Bank (Sveriges Riksbank) in memory of Nobel, leading to ongoing debates about its legitimacy. Unlike the natural sciences, economics is deeply intertwined with political ideology, and awarding a 'Nobel Prize' in economics lends significant credibility to theories that may be flawed or have negative real-world consequences. A striking example is the 1976 laureate, Milton Friedman, whose neoliberal economic policies – centred on deregulation, privatization, and monetarism – became highly influential. These ideas were implemented in Chile under dictator Augusto Pinochet, where the so-called Chicago Boys applied Friedman's theories, leading to severe

NOTES

economic inequality and suffering for millions. Critics argue that the prize often endorses ideological positions rather than objective scientific discoveries, raising fundamental questions about whether economics should be considered a science on par with physics or medicine and whether such a prize should exist at all.

4. The World Business Council for Sustainable Development (WBCSD) is a global coalition of leading companies that promotes sustainable business practices and corporate responsibility. It advocates for integrating environmental and social considerations into business strategies, emphasizing market-based solutions to sustainability challenges like climate change, resource management, and social equity. The WBCSD collaborates with governments, NGOs, and international organizations to influence policy and drive corporate sustainability initiatives. However, it faces criticism for being dominated by large multinational corporations, which some argue use sustainability rhetoric for greenwashing rather than enacting meaningful systemic change. Critics also point out that its market-driven approach may prioritize profit over deep structural transformations needed for true sustainability. See also: https://archive.corporateeurope.org/eurinc/chap2_8.html

5. Joseph Schumpeter disagreed with Marx and contemporary Marxist scholars on the relationship between capitalism, technology, and imperialism. He argued that the impulse for war and conquest was a remnant of pre-capitalist cultures, whereas capitalism inherently favours peace to facilitate business. For further discussion, see John E. King's article, 'Joseph Schumpeter and the Economics of Imperialism', published in Jacobin on 3 January 2022. https://jacobin.com/2022/01/joseph-schumpeter-economics-imperialism-marxism

6. Geoengineering, the large-scale manipulation of Earth's climate to counteract global warming, poses significant risks despite its potential benefits. Techniques like solar radiation management and carbon dioxide removal could have unintended consequences, including disrupting weather patterns, weakening monsoons, and harming ecosystems. Geoengineering might also create new geopolitical tensions, as different nations could be affected unequally, leading to conflicts over control and consequences. Additionally, reliance on these technologies could reduce pressure to cut emissions, prolonging dependence on fossil fuels rather than addressing the root causes of climate change. The lack of long-term testing and unknown side effects make geoengineering a highly risky and ethically complex approach to climate mitigation.

7. A recent report by Amnesty International titled 'The Occupation of Water' documents the systematic control or destruction of Palestinian

water sources by Israel forces and illegal settlers. https://www.amnesty.org/en/latest/campaigns/2017/11/the-occupation-of-water/. Systematic destruction of olive orchards is also very well documented: https://theecologist.org/2015/feb/25/arboricide-palestine-olive-orchard-destroyed

[8] Decolonize Palestine is an independent website created by Palestinian activists to provide resources, analysis, and historical context on the Palestinian struggle against Israeli occupation and settler colonialism. It aims to counter misinformation, challenge Zionist narratives, and offer decolonial perspectives on the conflict. The site includes articles, FAQs, myth-busting sections, and a library of resources to help people understand the realities of Palestinian resistance, history, and aspirations for liberation: https://decolonizepalestine.com/

[9] On 4 February 2025, President Trump in a press conference said: 'I don't think people should be going back to Gaza. Gaza is not a place for people to be living, and the only reason they want to go back, and I believe this strongly, is because they have no alternative ... If they had an alternative, they'd much rather not go back to Gaza and live in a beautiful alternative that's safe', https://www.theguardian.com/world/2025/feb/04/trump-netanyahu-gaza

two What's Wrong With Innovation and Why it Matters for a Post Growth Society

[1] https://www.somenergia.coop/es/

[2] Whig history (or Whig historiography) is an approach to historiography that presents history as a journey from an oppressive and benighted past to a 'glorious present'. The term was introduced by the British historian Herbert Butterfield in his book *The Whig Interpretation of History* of 1931. It takes its name from the British Whigs, advocates of the power of Parliament, who opposed the Tories, advocates of the power of the king. Butterfield referred to 'the nineteenth-century school of historiography that praised all progress and habitually associated Protestantism with liberal views of liberty'. The terms 'whig' and 'whiggish' are today commonly used to indicate 'universal descriptors for all progressive narratives'.

[3] A recent study published by *Nature* found that microplastics can accumulate in human brains (Nihart et al, 2025). The study analysed 91 brain tissue samples from autopsies and found that microplastic levels in the frontal cortex were up to 30 times greater than in the liver or kidneys. Notably, the brains of individuals diagnosed with dementia contained up to ten times more plastic particles, though the study did not establish a causal link between microplastics and dementia. Researchers suggest

possible mechanisms, such as obstructing blood flow or interfering with neural connections. Additionally, microplastic concentrations in the brain have increased by 50 per cent over the past eight years.
4   Ivan Illich's concept of convivial technology, introduced in the book *Tools for Conviviality*, refers to tools and systems that empower individuals and communities to exercise autonomy, creativity, and self-sufficiency rather than depending on large institutions or experts. In contrast to industrial and bureaucratic technologies, which Illich sees as alienating and controlling, convivial tools are adaptable, accessible, and designed to serve human needs without imposing rigid hierarchies. He outlines several dimensions of conviviality, including autonomy (the ability of individuals to use and modify tools freely), accessibility (ensuring that tools are available to all, not just experts or elites), flexibility (allowing tools to be used in multiple ways rather than enforcing rigid functions), and integrability (enabling technologies to complement, rather than replace, human skills and social relations). Illich argues that modern industrial society tends to create technologies that deskill people and centralize power, whereas convivial tools enable meaningful participation and personal agency. His vision promotes a balance where technology enhances human freedom rather than restricting it, supporting a more decentralized, sustainable, and just society.

three   Caring and Maintaining

1   See the platform https://repair.eu/
2   https://www.ifixit.com/

four   Organizations and Institutions for Post Growth

1   'Desobediencia Tecnológica. De la revolución al revolico' by Ernesto Oroza explores how Cubans adapted to technological scarcity through ingenuity and resourcefulness, particularly during the Período Especial – the economic crisis following the Soviet Union's collapse. Oroza examines how Cubans engaged in desobediencia tecnológica (technological disobedience), repurposing and hacking everyday objects to overcome shortages. This grassroots innovation often clashed with the state's efforts to control production and maintain ideological purity. The Cuban government, attempting to involve workers in decision-making, promoted collective input in production processes, yet its centralized model struggled to accommodate the spontaneous, unauthorized adaptations emerging from necessity. During the Período Especial, the government distributed manuals instructing citizens on how to repair and extend the life of household appliances and industrial machines,

acknowledging the need for decentralized, makeshift solutions. Oroza frames these survival-driven practices not just as economic adaptations but as a form of silent resistance, where citizens reclaimed agency over technology despite state restrictions. More info at: https://www.ernestooroza.com/desobediencia-tecnologica-de-la-revolucion-al-revolico/

[2] *Cosmolocalism* is a project funded by the European Research Council and led by Vasilis Kostakis at the Technical University of Tallin. The project explores how *cosmolocal* production models – which combine global knowledge sharing with local production – can create more sustainable and equitable economic systems. It examines how open-source technologies, peer-to-peer networks, and digital commons enable communities to access global design knowledge while using local resources for manufacturing. By analysing real-world case studies, the project investigates how *cosmolocalism* can challenge traditional capitalist production, promote environmental sustainability, and empower local communities through collaborative, decentralized innovation. More info available at: https://www.cosmolocalism.eu/

[3] https://coopcycle.org/

[4] Go-op proposes a public transport model owned by users and workers. More info at: https://go-op.coop/

[5] The Big Lemon encourages community-led transport. It publishes a guide called Community-Led Transport Initiatives, which it offers to anyone interested in setting up their own initiative. It also offers training and mentoring support. More info at: https://thebiglemon.com/

[6] https://www.thenews.coop/french-rail-operator-railcoop-goes-bust/

five The Infrastructural Conditions of Post Growth

[1] https://www.theguardian.com/technology/shortcuts/2019/mar/13/driverless-cars-racist

[2] IPv6 (Internet Protocol version 6) is the latest version of the Internet Protocol, used to identify and locate devices on networks and route traffic across the internet. It's the successor to IPv4, and a key difference is that IPv6 addresses are 128 bits long, compared to 32 bits for IPv4, providing a significantly larger address space.

six What Does it Mean Today to Democratize Technology?

[1] https://www.whitehouse.gov/remarks/2025/01/the-inaugural-address/

[2] AI is also at the centre of a sort of schizophrenic debate. On one hand, it is presented by the Trump-Musk administration as a tool to make

the state bureaucracy more efficient and freer from social progressive agendas. On the other, its risks are overstated, and people are primed to believe that AI constitutes an existential threat to humanity. This might automatically imply the need for a more centralized and authoritarian control. According to many analysts, this is the perfect recipes for techno-fascism. See also the article 'Anatomy of an AI coup' by Eryk Salvaggio: https://www.techpolicy.press/anatomy-of-an-ai-coup/

3 https://www.nytimes.com/2025/02/03/technology/musk-allies-ai-government.html

4 According to the EU, there are approximately 250,000 cooperatives across the EU, collectively owned by 163 million citizens. However, these cooperatives employ only 5.4 million people. The majority are concentrated in the agriculture, housing, and service sectors, with relatively few examples in manufacturing and technology-based industries. Notably, most cooperatives in Europe do not fully embrace democratic management and planning. In many cases, despite being formally structured as cooperatives, their internal labour relations closely resemble those of conventional wage-based employment.

5 The full story of the Lucas Plan can be found here: https://lucasplan.org.uk/story-of-the-lucas-plan/. In 1978 the Open University produced a short film, *The Story of the Lucas Aerospace Shop Stewards Alternative Corporate Plan*, available on YouTube: https://www.youtube.com/watch?v=C-3lZYT3izI&ab_channel=ResistanceTV. In 2018 the documentary *The Plan*, directed by Steve Sprung, was produced by Lx Filmes. Downloads available at: http://theplandocumentary.com/

6 https://www.common-wealth.org/

7 The documentary in Italian is available here: https://www.youtube.com/watch?v=s_Ty4n1W_dk

8 The project 'Rete Italiana delle Imprese Recuperate' (Italian network of recuperated companies) aims to create connection and share practices among workers of occupied or recuperated factories or companies. Italy has also a unique law (legge Marcora L. 49 del 27/02/1985) that created a special fund to support for the creation of coops through workers buyout or factories recoveries. More info available in Italian: https://impreserecuperate.comunet.online/new/output/pages/le-imprese.html

9 Rimaflow has also become a centre for political activism hosting events and promoting initiatives https://rimaflow.it/

10 An example is the Association for Progressive Communications, which advocates for a community-driven approach to internet ownership, emphasizing that access to the internet should be a public good rather than a commodity controlled by corporations. The association promotes decentralized, locally managed networks that empower communities,

particularly in underserved areas, to own, operate, and maintain their own internet infrastructure. This model fosters digital inclusion, affordability, and democratic control, ensuring that connectivity serves social justice, human rights, and sustainable development rather than purely commercial interests: https://www.apc.org/en/pubs/communal-internet-infrastructure

References

Abraham, Y. (2025) 'Israel developing ChatGPT-like tool that weaponizes surveillance of Palestinians', +972 Magazine, 6 March. Available from: https://www.972mag.com/israeli-intelligence-chatgpt-8200-surveillance-ai/ [Accessed 11 March 2025].

Albert, M.J. (2024) 'Growth hegemony and postgrowth futures: A complex hegemony approach', *Review of International Studies*, 50(5): 932–42.

Allan, B.B. (2018) *Scientific Cosmology and International Orders*, Cambridge University Press.

Anand, A., Argade, P., Barkemeyer, R. and Salignac, F. (2021) 'Trends and patterns in sustainable entrepreneurship research: A bibliometric review and research agenda', *Journal of Business Venturing*, 36(3): 106092.

Anderson, C. (2012) *Makers: The New Industrial Revolution*, Random House Business Books.

Andrieu, B., Vidal, O., Le Boulzec, H., Delannoy, L. and Verzier, F. (2022) 'Energy intensity of final consumption: The richer, the poorer the efficiency', *Environmental Science & Technology*, 56(19): 13909–19.

Asafu-Adjaye, J., Blomqvist, L., Brook, B.W., Ellis, E.C., Keith, D., Lynas, M. et al (2015) 'An ecomodernist manifesto'. Available from: http://ecite.utas.edu.au/107149

Avelino, F., Wittmayer, J.M., Pel, B., Weaver, P., Dumitru, A., Haxeltine, A. et al (2019) 'Transformative social innovation and (dis)empowerment', *Technological Forecasting and Social Change*, 145: 195–206.

Bakan, J. (2004) *Corporation: The Pathological Pursuit of Profit and Power*, Simon & Schuster.

Barlow, N., Regen, L., Cadiou, N., Chertkovskaya, E., Hollweg, M., Plank, C. et al (2022) *Degrowth & Strategy: How to Bring About Social-Ecological Transformation*, Mayfly Books.

Benkler, Y. (2016) 'Peer production, the commons, and the future of the firm', *Strategic Organization*, 15(2): 264–74.

Bessant, J., Lamming, R., Noke, H. and Phillips, W. (2005) 'Managing innovation beyond the steady state', *Technovation*, 25(12): 1366–76.

Bijker, W.E. (1995) *Bikes, Bakelite, and Bulbs: Steps Toward a Theory of Socio-Technical Change*, MIT Press.

Blum, A. (2012) *Tubes: A Journey to the Center of the Internet*, Ecco.

Bogliacino, F. and Pianta, M. (2010) 'Innovation and Employment: A Reinvestigation using Revised Pavitt classes', *Research Policy*, 39(6): 799–809.

Bollier, D. (2008) *Viral Spiral: How the Commoners Built a Digital Republic of their Own*, The New Press.

Bonaiuti, M. and Latouche, S. (2023) *La Grande Transizione. Il Declino della Civiltà Industriale e la Risposta della Decrescita*, Bollati Boringhieri.

Bookchin, M. (2004) *Post-Scarcity Anarchism*, AK Press.

Borrás, S. and Edler, J. (2020) 'The roles of the state in the governance of socio-technical systems' transformation', *Research Policy*, 49(5): 103971.

Bratton, B.H. (2016) *The Stack: On Software and Sovereignty*, MIT Press.

Brundtland, G.H. (1987) *Our Common Future: Report of the World Commission on Environment and Development*. Geneva, UN-Dokument A/42/427.

Bruni, L. and Zamagni, S. (2007) *Civil Economy: Efficiency, Equity, Public Happiness*, Peter Lang.

Bussu, S., Davis, H. and Pollard, A. (eds) (2014) *The Best of Sciencewise Reflections on Public Dialogue*, Sciencewise Byrd.

Callon, M. (1991) 'Techno-economic networks and irreversibility', in J. Law (ed) *A Sociology of Monsters: Essays on Power, Technology and Domination*, Routledge (Sociological Review Monographs), pp 132–61.

Carr, M. (1985) *The AT Reader: Theory and Practice in Appropriate Technology*, Intermediate Technology Publications.

Castoriadis, C. (1998) *The Imaginary Institution of Society*, MIT Press.

REFERENCES

Chen, X. and Kelly, T.F. (2015) 'B-Corps—A growing form of social enterprise', *Journal of Leadership & Organizational Studies*, 22(1): 102–14.

Cole, H.S.D. and Freeman, C. (1973) *Models of Doom: A Critique of the Limits to Growth*, Universe Pub.

Colombo, L.A., Bailey, A.R. and Gomes, M.V. (2023) 'Scaling in a postgrowth era: Learning from Social Agricultural Cooperatives', *Organization*: 13505084221147480.

Conde, M. and Walter, M. (2015) 'Commodity frontiers', in F.D. Giacomo D'Alisa Giorgios Kallis (ed) *Degrowth: A Vocabulary for a New Era*, Routledge, pp 71–4.

Cooley, M. (2020) *The Search for Alternatives: Liberating Human Imagination: A Mike Cooley Reader*, Spokesman.

Cozzens, S. and Kaplinsky, R. (2009) 'Innovation, poverty and inequality: cause, coincidence, or co-evolution?', in B.-A. Lundvall (ed) *Handbook of Innovation System and Developing Countries*, Edward Elgar, pp 57–82.

Cozzens, S. and Thakur, D. (2014) *Innovation and Inequality: Emerging Technologies in an Unequal World*, Edward Elgar.

Daly, H.E. (2008) *A Steady-State Economy – Report, Sustainable Development*, pp 1–10.

Darrow, K. and Pam, K. (1978) *Appropriate Technology Sourcebook*, Volunteers in Asia.

de la Bellacasa, M.P. (2017) *Matters of Care: Speculative Ethics in More than Human Worlds*, University of Minnesota Press.

Dentoni, D., Pascucci, S., Poldner, K. and Gartner, W.B. (2018) 'Learning "who we are" by doing: Processes of co-constructing prosocial identities in community-based enterprises', *Journal of Business Venturing*, 33(5): 603–22.

Devine, P. (1989) *Democracy and Economic Planning: The Political Economy of a Self-Governing Society*, Routledge.

Durrant, D. and Cohen, T. (2024) 'An infrastructural pathway to degrowth', *Democratic Theory*, 11(1): 92–115.

Edwards, M.G. (2021) 'The growth paradox, sustainable development, and business strategy', *Business Strategy and the Environment*, 30(7): 3079–94.

Ellul, J. (1964) *The Technological Society*, Vintage.

Escobar, A. (2004) 'Beyond the Third World: Imperial globality, global coloniality and anti-globalisation social movements', *Third World Quarterly*, 25(1): 207–30.

Fagerberg, J. and Verspagen, B. (2009) 'Innovation studies—The emerging structure of a new scientific field', *Research Policy*, 38(2): 218–33.

Feenberg, A. (1992) 'Subversive rationalization: Technology, power, and democracy', *Inquiry*, 35: 301–22.

Feenberg, A. (2001) *Transforming Technology: A Critical Theory Revisited*, Oxford University Press.

Feola, G. and Nunes, R. (2014) 'Success and failure of grassroots innovations for addressing climate change: The case of the Transition Movement', *Global Environmental Change*, 24(1): 232–50.

Fioramonti, L. (2013) *Gross Domestic Problem*, Zed Books.

Fisher, B. and Tronto, J. (2003) 'Toward a feminist theory of caring', in D. Cheal (ed) *Family: Critical Concepts in Sociology*, Psychology Press.

Fisher, M. (2009) *Capitalist Realism: Is There No Alternative?*, Zer0 Books.

Fitzpatrick, N., Parrique, T. and Cosme, I. (2022) 'Exploring degrowth policy proposals: A systematic mapping with thematic synthesis', *Journal of Cleaner Production*, 365: 132764.

Forti, V., Baldé, K. and Kuehr, R. (2018) E-waste statistics: Guidelines on classifications, reporting and indicators. United Nations University. Available from: https://www.greene.gov.in/wp-content/uploads/2020/12/2020120929.pdf

Fortuny-Sicart, A., Pansera, M. and Lloveras, J. (2024) 'Directing innovation through confrontation and democratisation: The case of platform cooperativism', *Journal of Responsible Innovation*, 11(1): 2414512.

Fressoli, M. and Dias, R. (2014) *The Social Technology Network: A Hybrid Experiment in Grassroots Innovation*, STEPS CENTRE University of Sussex.

REFERENCES

Frischmann, B.M. (2005) 'An economic theory of infrastructure and commons management', *Minnesota Law Review*, 673. Available from: https://scholarship.law.umn.edu/mlr/673

Geels, F.W. (2002) 'Technological transitions as evolutionary reconfiguration processes: A multi-level perspective and a case-study', *Research Policy*, 31(8–9): 1257–74.

Geels, F.W. (2005) 'The dynamics of transitions in socio-technical systems: A multi-level analysis of the transition pathway from horse-drawn carriages to automobiles (1860–1930)', *Technology Analysis & Strategic Management*, 17(4): 445–76.

Geels, F.W., Kern, F., Fuchs, G., Hinderer, N., Kungl, G., Mylan, J. et al (2016) 'The enactment of socio-technical transition pathways: A reformulated typology and a comparative multi-level analysis of the German and UK low-carbon electricity transitions (1990–2014)', *Research Policy*, 45(4): 896–913.

Genovese, A., Figueroa, A.A.A.A. and Koh, L.S.C. (2017) 'Sustainable supply chain management and the transition towards a circular economy: Evidence and some applications', *Omega*, 66: 344–57.

Gibson-Graham, J.K. (2006) *Postcapitalist Politics*, University of Minnesota Press.

Godin, B. (2020) *The Idea of Technological Innovation: A Brief Alternative History*, EE Elgar.

Godin, B. (2023) 'Withdrawal in the light of a historical analysis of innovation', in F. Goulet and D. Vinck (eds) *New Horizons for Innovation Studies: Doing Without, Doing With Less Destabilisation*, Edward Elgar.

Gomez-Baggethun, E. (2015) 'Commodification', in F.D. Giacomo D'Slisa Giorgios Kallis (ed) *Degrowth: A Vocabulary for a New Era*, Routledge, pp 67–70.

Gorz, A. (1980) *Ecology as Politics*, South End Press.

Goulet, F. and Vinck, D. (2023) *New Horizons for Innovation Studies*, Edward Elgar.

Gouveia, L. and Juska, A. (2002) 'Taming nature, taming workers: Constructing the separation between meat consumption and meat production in the U.S.', *Sociologia Ruralis*, 42(4): 370–90.

Graeber, D. (2007) *Possibilities: Essays on Hierarchy, Rebellion, and Desire*, AK Press.

Graeber, D. (2012) Of Flying Cars and the Declining Rate of Profit. *The Baffler No 19*. Available from: https://thebaffler.com/salvos/of-flying-cars-and-the-declining-rate-of-profit

Graeber, D. (2015) *The Utopia of Rules: On Technology, Stupidity, and the Secret Joys of Bureaucracy*, Melville House.

Graeber, D. and Wengrow, D. (2021) *The Dawn of Everything: A New History of Humanity*, Penguin UK.

Graziano, V. and Trogal, K. (2019) 'Repair matters', *Ephemera. Theory & Politics in Organization*, 19(2).

Guiltinan, J. (2009) 'Creative destruction and destructive creations: Environmental ethics and planned obsolescence', *Journal of Business Ethics*, 89(1): 19–28.

Harding, S. (ed) (2011) *The Postcolonial Science and Technology Studies Reader*, Duke University Press.

Hardt, L., Barrett, J., Taylor, P.G. and Foxon, T.J. (2021) 'What structural change is needed for a postgrowth economy: A framework of analysis and empirical evidence', *Ecological Economics*, 179: 106845.

Hargreaves, T., Hielscher, S., Seyfang, G. and Smith, A. (2013) 'Grassroots innovations in community energy: The role of intermediaries in niche development', *Global Environmental Change*, 23(5): 868–80.

Hekkert, M.P., Janssen, M.J., Wesseling, J.H. and Negro, S.O. (2020) 'Mission-oriented innovation systems', *Environmental Innovation and Societal Transitions*, 34: 76–9.

Hess, C. and Ostrom, E. (eds) (2007) *Understanding Knowledge as a Commons*, MIT Press.

Hickel, J., Kallis, G., Jackton, T., O'Neill, D.W., Schor, J.B., Steinberger, J.K. et al (2022) 'Degrowth can work — here's how science can help', *Nature*, 612(7940): 400–3.

Hickel, J. (2023) 'On technology and degrowth', *Monthly Review*, 75(3).

Hickel, J. and Kallis, G. (2019) 'Is Green Growth Possible?', *New Political Economy*: 1–18.

REFERENCES

Hielscher, S. and Smith, A.G. (2014) 'Community-based digital fabrication workshops: A review of the research literature', *SSRN Electronic Journal [Preprint]*.

Hughes, T.P. (1993) *Networks of Power: Electrification in Western Society, 1880–1930*, JHU Press.

Hughes, T.P. (2004) *Human-Built World: How to Think about Technology and Culture*, University of Chicago Press.

Illich, I. (1973) *Tools for Conviviality*, Harper & Row.

Illich, I. (1978) *The Right to Useful Unemployment and its Professional Enemies*.

Iraqi, A. (2024) '"Lavender": The AI machine directing Israel's bombing spree in Gaza, +972 Magazine'. Available from: https://www.972mag.com/lavender-ai-israeli-army-gaza/ [Accessed 10 December 2024].

Jackson, S.J. (2014) 'Rethinking Repair', in T. Gillespie, P.J. Boczkowski and K.A. Foot, *Media Technologies: Essays on Communication, Materiality, and Society*, MIT Press.

Jackson, T. (2009) *Prosperity without growth? The transition to a sustainable economy*, Sustainable Development Commission, p 136.

Jasanoff, S. and Kim, S. (2015) *Dreamscapes of Modernity: Sociotechnical Imaginaries and the Fabrication of Power*, University of Chicago Press.

Jasanoff, S. and Kim, S.-H. (2009) 'Containing the atom: Sociotechnical imaginaries and nuclear power in the United States and South Korea', *Minerva*, 47(2): 119–46.

Jimenez, A., Pansera, M. and Abdelnour, S. (2025) 'Imposing innovation: How "innovation speak" maintains postcolonial exclusion in Peru', *World Development*, 189: 106914.

Joerges, B. (1999) 'Do politics have artefacts?', *Social Studies of Science*, 29(3): 411–31.

Jossa, B. (2018) *A New Model of Socialism: Democratising Economic Production*, Edward Elgar.

Jünger, F.G. (1949) *The Failure of Technology: Perfection Without Purpose*, Henry Regnery Company.

Kallis, G. (2011) 'In defence of degrowth', *Ecological Economics*, 70(5): 873–80.

Kallis, G. (2018) *Degrowth*, Agenda Publishing.

Kallis, G. (2019) *Limits: Why Malthus Was Wrong and Why Environmentalists Should Care*, Stanford University Press.

Kallis, G. (2021) 'Limits, ecomodernism and degrowth', *Political Geography*, 87: 102367.

Kallis, G. et al (2025) 'Postgrowth: The science of wellbeing within planetary boundaries', *The Lancet Planetary Health*, 9(1): e62–e78.

Kallis, G. and March, H. (2015) 'Imaginaries of hope: The utopianism of degrowth', *Annals of the Association of American Geographers*, 105(2): 360–8.

Kaplinsky, R. (2011) 'Schumacher meets Schumpeter: Appropriate technology below the radar', *Research Policy*, 40(2): 193–203.

Kasmir, S. (1999) 'The Mondragon model as post-Fordist discourse: Considerations on the production of post-Fordism', *Critique of Anthropology*, 19(4): 379–400.

Keen, S. (2021) 'The appallingly bad neoclassical economics of climate change', *Globalizations*, 18(7): 1149–77.

Kerschner, C., Wächter, P., Nierling, L. and Ehlers, M.-H. (2018) 'Degrowth and technology: Towards feasible, viable, appropriate and convivial imaginaries', *Journal of Cleaner Production*, 197(2): 1619–36.

Kirwan, J., Ilbery, B. Maye, D. and Carey, J. (2013) 'Grassroots social innovations and food localisation: An investigation of the Local Food programme in England', *Global Environmental Change*, 23(5): 830–7.

Kitchin, R. and Fraser, A. (2020) *Slow Computing*, Bristol University Press.

Latouche, S. (2009) *Farewell to Growth*, Polity Press.

Latour, B. (2011) 'Love your monsters: Why we must care for our technologies as we do our children – Google search', *Breakthrough Journal*, 2(11): 21–8.

Leonardi, E. and Gabbriellini, F. (2023) 'La just transition come strategia partecipativa del lavoro: sapere operaio e democrazia economica nella vertenza ex GKN', *Economia e Società Regionale*, 3: 53–72.

Lepawsky, J. (2018) *Reassembling Rubbish: Worlding Electronic Waste*, MIT Press.

REFERENCES

Leydesdorff, L. (2000) 'The triple helix: an evolutionary model of innovations', *Research Policy*, 29(2): 243–55.

Llorente-González, L.J. and Vence, X. (2020) 'How labour-intensive is the circular economy? A policy-orientated structural analysis of the repair, reuse and recycling activities in the European Union', *Resources, Conservation and Recycling*, 162: 105033.

Lloveras, J., Marshall, A.P., Warnaby, G. and Kalandides, A. (2021) 'Mobilising sense of place for degrowth? Lessons from Lancashire's anti-fracking activism', *Ecological Economics*, 183: 106754.

Lloveras, J., Marshall, A.P., Vandeventer, J.P. and Pansera, M. (2022) 'Sustainability marketing beyond sustainable development: Towards a degrowth agenda', *Journal of Marketing Management*, 38(17–18): 2055–77.

Lloveras, J., Pansera, M. and Smith, A. (2024) 'On "the politics of repair beyond repair": Radical democracy and the Right to Repair movement', *Journal of Business Ethics [Preprint]*.

Loewenstein, A. (2023) *The Palestine Laboratory: How Israel Exports the Technology of Occupation Around the World*, Verso.

Lundvall, B. (ed) (2010) *National Systems of Innovation: Toward a Theory of Innovation and Interactive Learning*, Anthem Press.

Macnaghten, P. and Owen, R. (2011) 'Good governance for geoengineering', *Nature*, 479(7373).

Martin, C.J. (2016) 'The sharing economy: A pathway to sustainability or a nightmarish form of neoliberal capitalism?', *Ecological Economics*, 121: 149–59.

Martinez-Alier, J. (2002) *The Environmentalism of the Poor: A Study of Ecological Conflicts and Valuation*, Edward Elgar.

Mastrandrea, A. (2015) *Lavoro Senza Padroni: Storie di Operai che Fanno Rinascere Imprese*, Baldini & Castoldi.

Matchar, E. (2016) 'The Fight for the "Right to Repair"', the Smithsonian. Available from: https://www.smithsonianmag.com/innovation/fight-right-repair-180959764/

Mattei, U. (2011) *Beni Comuni: Un Manifesto*, Laterza.

May, C. (2015) *The Global Political Economy of Intellectual Property Rights* (2nd ed), Routledge.

Mazzucato, M. and Perez, C. (2023) 'Redirecting growth: Inclusive, sustainable and innovation-led', in E.S. Reinert and I.H. Kvangraven (eds) *A Modern Guide to Uneven Economic Development*, EE Elgar, pp 71–106.

McQuillan, D. (2022) *Resisting AI: An Anti-fascist Approach to Artificial Intelligence*, Bristol University Press.

McRobie, G. (1981) *Small Is Possible*, Abacus.

Meadows, D. and Randers, J. (2006) *Limits to Growth: The 30-Year Update* (Vol. 43), Chelsea Green Publishing Co.

Miller, C. (2022) *Chip War: The Fight for the World's Most Critical Technology*, Scribner.

Moellendorf, D. (2022) *Mobilizing Hope: Climate Change and Global Poverty*, Oxford University Press.

Mumford, L. (1964) 'Authoritarian and Democratic Technics', *Technology and Culture*, 5(1): 1–8.

Nakano, Y. (2010) 'On Serge Latouche's theories of post-development and degrowth [translator's postscript]（セルジュ・ラトゥーシュの思想圏について）', in Can we have prosperity without growth? Towards an economics of degrowth and post-development（経済成長なき社会発展は可能か？〈脱成長〉と〈ポスト開発〉の経済学), Sakuhinsha Publishing Inc., pp 277–338.

Nihart, A.J., Garcia, M.A., el Hayek, E., Liu, R., Olewine, M., Kingston, J.D. et al (2025) 'Bioaccumulation of microplastics in decedent human brains', *Nature Medicine*, 31: 1114–19.

OECD (2021) Public Sector Innovation Facets MISSION-ORIENTED INNOVATION. OECD. Available from: https://oecd-opsi.org/wp-content/uploads/2021/10/OECD-Innovation-Facets-Brief-Mission-Oriented-Innovation-2021.pdf

Ornetzeder, M. and Rohracher, H. (2013) 'Of solar collectors, wind power, and car sharing: Comparing and understanding successful cases of grassroots innovations', *Global Environmental Change*, 23(5): 856–67.

Oroza, E. (2019) 'Desobediencia tecnologica'. Available from: http://www.ernestooroza.com/tag/desobediencia-tecnologica/

REFERENCES

Owen, R., Pansera, M., Macnaghten, P. and Randles, S. (2021) 'Organisational institutionalisation of responsible innovation', *Research Policy*, 50(1): 104–32.

Pansera, M. and Fressoli, M. (2021) 'Innovation without growth: Frameworks for understanding technological change in a postgrowth era', *Organization*, 28(3): 380–404.

Pansera, M., Lloveras, J. and Durrant, D. (2024) 'The infrastructural conditions of (de-)growth: The case of the internet', *Ecological Economics*, 215: 108001.

Pansera, M. and Owen, R. (2018a) 'Framing inclusive innovation within the discourse of development: Insights from case studies in India', *Research Policy*, 47(1): 23–34.

Pansera, M. and Owen, R. (2018b) *Innovation and Development: The Politics at the Bottom of the Pyramid*, ISTE-Wiley.

Pansera, M. and Rizzi, F. (2020) 'Furbish or perish: Italian social cooperatives at a crossroads', *Organization*, 27(1): 17–35.

Papadimitropoulos, V. (2024) 'The digital commons, cosmolocalism, and open cooperativism: The cases of P2P Lab and Tzoumakers', *Organization*, 31(6): 970–93.

Parker, M., Cheney, G., Fournier, V. and Land, C. (eds) (2014) *The Routledge Companion to Alternative Organization*, Routledge.

Parrique, T. et al (2019) Decoupling Debunked. Evidence and arguments against green growth as a sole strategy for sustainability. A study edited by the European Environment Bureau EEB. Available from: https://eeb.org/library/decoupling-debunked/

Peredo, A.M. and Chrisman, J.J. (2006) 'Toward a Theory of Community-Based Enterprise', *Academy of Management Review*, 31(2): 309–28.

Perez, C. (2019) 'Transitioning to smart green growth: lessons from history', in R. Fouquet (ed) *Handbook on Green Growth*, Edward Elgar.

Perzanowski, A. (2022) *The Right to Repair: Reclaiming the Things We Own*, Cambridge University Press.

Pfotenhauer, S. et al (2022) 'The politics of scaling', *Social Studies of Science*, 52(1): 3–34.

Pfotenhauer, S.M., Juhl, J. and Aarden, E. (2019) 'Challenging the "deficit model" of innovation: Framing policy issues under the innovation imperative', *Research Policy*, 48(4): 895–904.

Pianta, M. (2006) 'Innovation and Employment', in J. Fagerberg and D.C. Mowery (eds) *The Oxford Handbook of Innovation*, Oxford University Press.

Pighetti, F., Papaleo, I. and Izzo, L. (2009) Da classe operaia a classe dirigente. La cooperativa Megaride, un'impresa dei lavoratori. La Citta del Sole. Available from: https://www.ibs.it/da-classe-operaia-a-classe-libro-vari/e/9788882924492?srsltid=AfmBOoqPs4sKLtR3eFC8VnekU9swxNRKlcPh8aEzXjHu-UF2kGzQQvxb [Accessed 31 January 2025].

Piketty, T. (2014) *Capital in the Twenty-First Century*, Harvard University Press.

Polanyi, K. (2001) *The Great Transformation: The Political and Economic Origins of Our Time*, Beacon Press.

Poledrini, S. (2014) 'Unconditional reciprocity and the case of Italian social cooperatives', *Nonprofit and Voluntary Sector Quarterly*, 44(3): 457–73.

Prabhu N, S. and Majhi, R. (2023) 'Disposal of obsolete mobile phones: A review on replacement, disposal methods, in-use lifespan, reuse and recycling', *Waste Management & Research*, 41(1): 18–36.

Purpose Foundation (2022) Steward-Ownership: Rethinking ownership in the 21st century Resource. Available from: https://embeddingproject.org/resources/steward-ownership-rethinking-ownership-in-the-21st-century/ [Accessed 11 March 2025].

Radjou, N., Prabhu, J. and Ahuja, S. (2012) *Jugaad Innovation: Think Frugal, Be Flexible, Generate Breakthrough Growth*, Jossey-Bass.

Rätzer, M., Hartz, R. and Winkler, I. (2018) 'Editorial: Postgrowth organizations', *Management Revue*, 29(3): 193–205.

Raworth, K. (2017) *Doughnut Economics: Seven Ways to Think Like a 21st-Century Economist*. Chelsea Green Publishing.

Richardson, K., Steffen, W., Lucht, W., Bendtsen, J., Cornell, S.E., Donges, J.F. et al (2023) 'Earth beyond six of nine planetary boundaries', *Science Advances*, 9(37).

REFERENCES

Riechmann, J. (2022) *El Socialismo Puede Llegar Sólo en Bicicleta*, Catarata.

Rist, G. (2011) *The History of Development: From Western Origins to Global Faith* (3rd ed), Zed Books.

Ritzer, G. and Jurgenson, N. (2010) 'Production, consumption, prosumption', *Journal of Consumer Culture*, 10(1): 13–36.

Robra, B. et al (2023) 'From creative destruction to convivial innovation – A postgrowth perspective', *Technovation*, 125: 102760.

Rogaly, K. (2024) 'A Lucas Plan for the Twenty First Century From Asset Manager Arsenal to Green Industrial Strategy', commonwealth.org. Available from: https://cdn.prod.website-files.com/62306a0b42f386df612fe5b9/6710de5a4201df8a7cfaa08d_A%20Lucas%20Plan%20for%20the%20Twenty%20First%20Century.pdf

Romano, O. (2015) 'Depense', in G. D'Alisa, F. Demaria and Kallis, G. (eds) *Degrowth: A Vocabulary for a New Era*, Routledge.

Rosa, H. (2019) *Resonance: A Sociology of Our Relationship to the World*, John Wiley & Sons, Inc.

Rowland, N.J. and Passoth, J.-H. (2015) 'Infrastructure and the state in science and technology studies', *Social Studies of Science*, 45(1): 137–45.

Russell, B. (1997) *In Praise of Idleness: And Other Essays*, Routledge.

Sachs, W. (ed) (2010) *The Development Dictionary*, Zed Books.

Santo, M.K.D. (2024) 'Yugoslav self-management: The forgotten anti-capitalist seeds of degrowth', *Cultura Económica*, 42(108): 50–85.

Savini, F. (2019) 'The economy that runs on waste: Accumulation in the circular city', *Journal of Environmental Policy and Planning*, 21(6): 675–91.

Savini, F. (2024) 'Post-Growth, Degrowth, the Doughnut, and Circular Economy: A Short Guide for Policymakers', *Journal of City Climate Policy and Economy*, 2(2): 113–23.

Scholz, T. (2016) Platform Cooperativism: Challenging the Corporate Sharing Economy. Rosa Luxemburg Stiftung. Available from: https://rosalux.nyc/wp-content/uploads/2020/11/RLS-NYC_platformcoop.pdf [Accessed 16 June 2023].

Schot, J. and Steinmueller, W.E. (2018) 'Three frames for innovation policy: R&D, systems of innovation and transformative change', *Research Policy*, 47(9): 1554–67.

Schramm, E., Lloveras, J. and Pansera, M. (2024) 'Transport innovations in the cracks: reading for potential postgrowth transport and mobilities with Deleuze and Guattari', *Local Environment*: 1–22.

Schumacher, E.F. (1973) *Small is Beautiful*, Harper & Row.

Schumpeter, J.A. (1934) *The Theory of Economic Development: An Inquiry into Profits, Capital, Credit, Interest, and the business Cycle* (Harvard University Press), Transaction Publishers.

Schumpeter, J.A. (1994) *Capitalism, Socialism and Democracy*, Routledge.

Serres, M. (1995) *The Natural Contract*, University of Michigan Press.

Seyfang, G. and Haxeltine, A. (2012) 'Growing grassroots innovations: Exploring the role of community-based initiatives in governing sustainable energy transitions', *Environment and Planning C: Government and Policy*, 30(3): 381–400.

Shove, E. and Trentmann, F. (2018) *Infrastructures in Practice: The Dynamics of Demand in Networked Societies*, Routledge.

Smith, A. (2005) 'The alternative technology movement: An analysis of its framing and negotiation of technology development', *Human Ecology*, 12(2): 106–19.

Smith, A. and Ely, A. (2015) 'Green transformation from below? The politics of grassroots innovation', in I. Scoones, M. Leach, and P. Newell (eds) *The Politics of Green Transformations*, Routledge.

Smith, A. and Ely, A. (2025) 'From limits to growth to postgrowth: The international politics of technology in historical perspective', *Science, Technology and Society*, forthcoming.

Smith, A. and Fressoli, M. (2021) 'Post-automation', *Futures*, 132: 102778.

Smith, A., Fressoli, M. and Thomas, H. (2014) 'Grassroots innovation movements: Challenges and contributions', *Journal of Cleaner Production*, 63(1): 114–24.

Solow, R.M. (1974) 'The economics of resources or the resources of economics', *The American Economic Review*, 64(2): 1–14.

REFERENCES

Solow, R.M. (2002) Interview with Robert Solow. *The Region*. Available from: http://www.minneapolisfed.org/publications_papers/pub_display.cfm?id=3399&TC=1

Soper, K. (2020) *Postgrowth Living: For an Alternative Hedonism*, Verso.

Star, S.L. (1999) 'The ethnography of infrastructure', *American Behavioral Scientist*, 43(3): 377–91.

Steffen, W., Broadgate, W., Deutsch, L.M., Gaffney, O. and Ludwig, C. (2015) 'The trajectory of the Anthropocene: The Great Acceleration', *The Anthropocene Review*, 2(1): 81–98.

Stirling, A. (2008) '"Opening up" and "closing down" power, participation, and pluralism in the social appraisal of technology', *Science, Technology, & Human Values*, 33(2): 262–94.

Stirling, A. (2015) 'Towards innovation democracy? Participation, responsibility and precaution in the politics of science and technology', in STEPS Working Paper 78. STEPS Centre Brighton. Available from: https://steps-centre.org/wp-content/uploads/Innovation-Democracy.pdf

Storey, J., Basterretxea, I. and Salaman, G. (2014) 'Managing and resisting "degeneration" in employee-owned businesses: A comparative study of two large retailers in Spain and the United Kingdom', *Organization*, 21(5): 626–44.

Strand, R., Saltelli, A., Giampietro, M., Rommetveit, K. and Funtowicz, S. (2018) 'New narratives for innovation', *Journal of Cleaner Production*, 197: 1849–53.

Surowiecki, J. (2004) *The Wisdom of Crowds*, Anchor Books.

The Invisible Committee (2017) Now. Semiotext(e).

Thomas, A. (2004) 'The Rise of Social Cooperatives in Italy', *VOLUNTAS: International Journal of Voluntary and Nonprofit Organizations*, 15(3): 243–63.

Todaro, R. and Arriagada, I. (2020) 'Global Care Chains', in N.A. Naples (ed) *Companion to Women's and Gender Studies*, John Wiley & Sons, Inc., pp 347–64.

Uyarra, E., Ribeiro, B. and Dale-Clough, L. (2019) 'Exploring the normative turn in regional innovation policy: Responsibility and the quest for public value', *European Planning Studies*, 27(12): 2359–75.

van den Bergh, J.C.J.M. (2011) 'Environment versus growth — A criticism of "degrowth" and a plea for "a-growth"', *Ecological Economics*, 70(5): 881–90.

Vetter, A., Schmelzer, M. and Vansintjan, A. (2023) *The Future Is Degrowth: A Guide to a World Beyond Capitalism*, Verso.

Victor, P.A. (2008) *Managing Without Growth: Slower by Design, Not Disaster*, Edward Elgar Publishing.

Vinsel, L. and Russell, A.L. (2020) *The Innovation Delusion*, Penguin Random House.

Vogel, J. and Hickel, J. (2023) 'Is green growth happening? An empirical analysis of achieved versus Paris-compliant CO_2–GDP decoupling in high-income countries', *The Lancet Planetary Health*, 7(9): e759–69.

War on Want (2015) 'TTIP, CETA, TISA and public services'. Available from: https://waronwant.org/media/ttip-ceta-tisa-and-public-services

Weber, S. (2005) *The Success of Open Source*, Harvard University Press.

Weisman, A. (2008) *The World Without Us*, Ebury Publishing.

Western, B. (1995) 'A comparative study of working-class disorganization: Union decline in eighteen advanced capitalist countries', *American Sociological Review*, 60(2): 179–201.

Winner, L. (1978) *Autonomous Technology*, MIT Press.

Winner, L. (1980) 'Do Artefacts Have Politics?', *Daedalus*, 109(1): 121–36.

Winner, L. (1993) 'Upon opening the black box and finding it empty: Social constructivism of technology the philosophy of technology', *Science, Technology, & Human Values*, 18(3): 362–78.

Winner, L. (2004) 'Technology as forms of life', in D.M. Kaplan, *Readings in the Philosophy of Technology*, Rowman & Littlefield [Preprint].

Zizek, S. (2011) *Living in the End Times*, Verso Books.

Index

References to endnotes show both the page number and the note number (143n4), and where required for clarity, the chapter number (ch1).

A

accessibility 12, 61, 89, 102, 143n4
accountability 45, 55
African cities, informal repair economies 51
agroecology 72
AI systems 14, 29–30, 111, 112, 135, 144–5n2
Airbnb 87
Albert, M.J. 6
Allan, B. 7–8
alternative economies 85
alternative production networks 132
alternative supply chains 132
Amnesty International 141–2n7
appropriate technology 47, 68, 69, 70
Association for Progressive Communications 145–6n10
Athens 112
authoritarian rule 113
automation 42, 43
automobility 36–7
autonomy 70, 84, 85, 131, 143n4

B

backmarket 59
backstop technology 17, 140n2
Bakan, J. 120
Bariloche model 19–20
Barlow, N. 127–8
Bellacasa, Puig de la 55–6
bicycles 88–91
Big Lemon, The 76–7, 144n5
biodigesters 71

Bonaiuti, M. 18
Bookchin, M. 46
Borrás, S. 119
Bratton, B.H. 104
Brazil 71, 72, 82
broken world thinking 52
Brundtland Report 21
Butterfield, H. 142n2

C

capitalism 103, 107, 109
  capitalist system 27
  critique of 118–21
  free market 21, 25, 48
  late-stage 14
  modern 51
  and technology 127–8
  undemocratic nature of labour under 127–8
capitalist realism 8, 134, 136
carbon taxation 128
care 56
  burden of 57
  and collective wisdom 56
  concept of 129
  as democratic project 56–7
  division of labour 57
  and gender 57
  innovation as 54–6
  politics of 56–7
  productive vs reproductive 57
  speculative ethics 56
Castoriadis, C. 139–40n3
centralization 85
Chicago Boys 140n3(ch1)
Chile 140n3(ch1)
circular economy 96

cisternas de placa 71
citizen science 73
citizens' audits 127
civil economy 72
climate change 5, 13, 18, 28, 107
Cohen, T. 92
Cold War 35
collaboration 68, 84
collaborative production *see* open and collaborative production
collaborative value creation 86
collapse scenario (internet) 108
collective imagination 139n3
collective welfare 33–4, 43
Colombo 84, 97
colonial domination through technology 39
coltan mining 11, 14, 26
commodification 80, 83, 85
common-based peer production 73, 83
commons (as concept) 127
commons-based infrastructures 99
commons-based production 127, 129
communitarian repair frame 61
community economies 85
community energy projects 70
community-based enterprises 73
community-led initiatives 131
Community-Led Transport Initiatives 144n5
community-supported agriculture 127
complexity and simplicity 90
Comprehensive Economic and Trade Agreement 83
consumer rights frame 60
context-sensitive approaches 70
control, illusion of 11, 31, 35, 43–5, 134
convivial tools/technology 6, 11, 47, 83, 94–5, 109, 127, 143n4
Cooley, M. 122, 126
CoopCycle 74–6, 80, 83, 136–7
cooperatives 68, 72, 86, 123–4, 127, 129, 131, 136

collective ownership 74, 132
cooperative model 74–5
 governance structures 81–2
 Mondragon Corporation 86
 multiplication and replication 84
 social cooperatives 72, 82
 surplus management 82
co-optation 87
coproduction 86
copyleft licence 75
corporate hierarchies 121
corporate power 120–1
cosmolocalism 73, 144n2(ch4)
cosmology of progress 7
creative destruction 11, 24, 25, 37–8, 54
creativity 23, 136
critical theory of technology 40
critical thinking 116
Cuba 51, 71, 143n1(ch4)
cultural revolution 6

D

Daly, H. 33
data centres 103, 104, 106, 108, 109
 energy consumption 105
 refrigeration 107
decentralization 73, 85
decision-making, collective 116
Decolonize Palestine 142n8
decoupling 2, 4, 11, 18, 20, 139n2
degrowth 3–4, 9–10, 40, 86, 120
 dual infeasibility 4–5
 innovation policy 126–33
 organizational models 131–2
 political miracle 5
 strategic thinking 127–8
 and technology 47–8
 see also post growth
dematerialization 18
democratic governance
 of infrastructures 92, 109
 of technology 41, 47, 48, 64
democratization
 economic 138
 of production 136, 137
 of technology 114–17, 129

INDEX

digital initiatives 87
digital platforms 115
digital technologies 44, 98
disposability, culture of 55
DIY movements 71
downscaling technologies 87
dual infeasibility 4–5
Durrant, D. 92

E

e-bikes 89
ecocide 11, 26, 27, 30, 31
ecology of tools 46
eco-modernism 2, 10, 139n2
economic and environmental objectives, integration of 2
economic growth 14, 68, 80, 85, 86
  abandonment as goal 4
  critique of 32–3, 118–20
  directed to social problems 20
  and innovation 15–21
  religion of 10
  as utopian project 33
economic planning 120
Edler, J. 119
electric cars 115
electric grids 94, 102–3
electric vehicle batteries 27
electronic waste 53
Ellul, J. 46, 117, 126
employment
  automation and job losses 42
  and innovation 41–2
energy efficiency 108
energy industry 37
England 37
environmental frame 60
environmental movements 17
epistemicide 11, 26, 28, 30, 31
epistemological plurality 87
essential services, cooperative ownership of 132
ethnic cleansing 29
Europe 37, 137

European Repair Information Form 62
European Research Council 144n2(ch4)
European Union 23, 118, 145n4
exclusion, technological 115
export-driven production 81

F

fab labs 11, 73, 81
FabLab 73
factor productivity 82
fairphone 59
family-run businesses 114
Feenberg, A. 39, 40, 115, 116, 135
financialization of internet infrastructure 107
Fisher, M. 8, 134
Fitzpatrick, N. 127
flexibility 143n4
fogões ecológicos 71
food networks 70
fossil fuels 44–5, 130
France 77
Fraser, A. 136
free market 21, 25, 48
Fressoli, M. 97, 98
Friedman, M. 140n3(ch1)

G

Galaxy Zoo 74
Gaza 13, 142n9
GDP 14
Geels, F.W. 96, 100, 101
Genoa bridge collapse (2018) 52
genocide 11, 26, 28, 30, 31
geoengineering 5, 27, 127, 141n6
geopolitical interests 86
Gibson-Graham, J.K. 85
gig economy 44
GKN factory, Florence 125
Global North 93
Global South 3, 39
GMOs 127
Godin, B. 22, 23

Google
  driverless cars 93
  Dunant cable 104–5
Go-op 76, 144n4
Gorz, A. 6, 32, 42–3, 46, 57, 126, 139n1
Goulet, D. 117
Goulet, F. 136
governance structures 72, 81–2
Graeber, D. 112, 116, 134, 136, 137–8
grand civilizational projects 7
grassroots environmental movements 130
grassroots innovations 38, 60–1, 68, 70, 71, 84, 87, 143n1(ch4)
Graziano, V. 56
Greece 73, 80, 81
'green' energy projects 27
green growth 2, 4, 20, 21
green marketing 9
Green New Deal 128
green technologies 20–1
growth hegemony 6–7
growth paradigm 101, 107–8
  alternatives to 33–4
  fading promises 32–3
growth realism 8–9
growth-oriented organizations 68
  characteristics 78–84
  and post-growth, comparison 78–84
guilds 136
Gujarat, India 38, 39
Gupta, A. 38

H

Harding, S. 26
Heidegger, M. 117, 126
Hekkert, M.P. 119
Hickel, J. 88
hierarchical organizations 114
high-tech approaches, Western-centric 38–9
Honey Bee Network 38, 70
hope and optimism 10
Horizon 2020 (European Union) 23
housing 110
Howard, E. 97
Hughes, T.P. 95–6, 100, 101–3
human ingenuity 36, 139n2
humanity, reconciliation with limits 8
hydroelectric dams 28

I

ICT sector emissions 105
iFixit 71
Illich, I. 6, 11, 47, 70, 83, 88, 94–5, 126, 143n4
illiteracy programs 38
imperialism 86
India 51, 70
indigenous communities 28, 30
indigenous knowledge 28
inequalities, social 50, 53, 57, 63–4
inequality
  distributive effects 41
  and innovation 41–3
infrastructure 50–1
  collapse of 108
  commons-based 99
  consolidation and expansion 100
  and convivial tools 109
  decommissioning 130
  democratic governance of 92, 109
  democratization 130
  design for growth 100–7
  and embedded politics 92–3
  fragility of 52
  futures of 107–10
  growth dependency of 105–7
  hybrid management approaches 132
  mega-infrastructures 110
  neglect of 52–3
  power embedded in 99
  publicly governed 99
  regional 97–8

INDEX

repurposing of 109
sacrifice zones 109
social construction of 92–4
sociotechnical landscapes 100–1
under-investment in 52–3
urban 99
innovation
  alternative modes of 85, 86, 87
  for better growth 24
  capability 24
  as care 54–6
  care, repair, and democratic participation 11–12
  as caring 48
  creative destruction 54
  critique of mainstream narrative 34–5
  ecosystems 22
  employment effects 41–2
  grassroots *see* grassroots innovations
  and growth 15–21, 34
  imperatives 22–3
  implicit assumptions 31
  'innovate or die' imperative 21–4, 34
  innovation speak 21
  mania 31
  market orientation 22
  market-driven 22–3
  mission-oriented 118–21
  non-growth-oriented 85
  plural and conditional nature 45–6
  post-growth policy 63–6, 126–33
  repoliticization of 45–7
  research implications 85
  responsible innovation 45, 130
  seamless, myth of 50–2
  systems theory 31
  technological determinism 11
  ungoverned innovation 43–5
integrability 143n4
intellectual property 59, 63, 79, 83
internet 103–9
  bandwidth 107
  collapse scenario 108
  data centres 105, 107
  financialization of 107
  growth dependency 105–7
  logical layer 106–7
  physical layer 104–5, 107
  sober scenario 108–9
  'stack' 104, 108
  submarine cables 104–7, 109
  traffic 105
Internet Protocol 144n2(ch5)
Invisible Committee, The 99
Israel 29–30
Italy 72, 124–5, 145n8

J

Jackson, S. 52, 63
Jobim, A. C. 136
jugaad 51
Jünger, E. 46

K

Kallis, G. 128, 140n3(int)
Kitchin, R. 136
Kivu, Congo 14
knowledge
  commons 81
  democratization of 85
  erasure *see* epistemicide
  exchange 84
  indigenous 87
  local 87
  production 81
Kostakis, V. 144n2(ch4)

L

labour movement 125
large technical systems 101–2
Latin America 70
Latouche, S. 96, 139n1
Latour, B. 55, 64
Lavender system 29–30
Le Guin, U.K. 43
liberatory technology 46
Limits to Growth 6, 11, 17, 18, 19, 20

Linux operating system 73–4, 82, 98
load factors 102
local alternatives 129
local autonomy 85
local empowerment 68, 72, 73
local solutions 39
localism, and scale 97
Loewenstein, A. 29
logical layer (internet) 106–7
Long Island bridges 92–3
'Love Your Monsters' (Latour) 55
low-tech infrastructure 128
low-tech movement 109
Lucas Plan 121–3, 125, 137
Luddism 48

M

Macnaghten, P. 43–4, 45
maintenance 50–2
  as boring 50
  costs of neglect of 52–4
  labour of 51, 65
  undervaluation of 50–1, 65
Maison des Coursiers 75
makers' movements 71, 83
makerspaces 11, 73, 81
marginalized voices 30
market competition 34
Mazzucato, M. 21, 118, 120
Meadows, D. 18, 19, 21
mega-infrastructures 110
Megaride cooperative, Italy 123–5
microelectronics 86
microplastics 142–3n3
military interests 86
military spending 6
military-industrial complex 110
Miller, C. 29
mobile phones 26
mobility solutions 90
Models of Doom (Cole and Feeman) 18–19, 21
modularity 98
Moellendorf, D. 10
Mondragon Corporation 86

monetary systems 110
monopolies, corporate 58–9, 63
monopolization, resisting 129
moral corruption 15
Morandi Bridge 52
Moses, R. 92–3
multinational corporations 68, 83, 86
Musk, E. 111, 112

N

national security 6
nationalization 137
nation-states 86
naturalization of technological paths 36
negative trends 24, 26
neoclassical economics 18
neoliberal counter-revolution 20
neoliberalism 116, 120
net-zero initiatives 5
Nobel, A. 140n3(ch1)
non-market solutions 81
Nordhaus, W. 17, 18, 140n2
novelty, valorization of 51, 54
nowtopias 95, 128
nuclear plants 110
nuclear power 127, 130

O

obsolescence 53, 58, 64
OECD 21, 22, 23, 118
oligopolies 84
Oliver, J. 50
open and collaborative production 68, 73–4, 84, 87
open hardware 73
open licences 74
open source
  communities 81
  Linux 73–4, 82
  movement 73
  platforms 12
  software 73
  technologies 98

INDEX

Organisation for Economic Co-operation and Development (OECD) 11
organizations 67, 129, 131–2
  alternative organizational forms 86
  community-based enterprises 73
  cooperative *see* cooperatives
  distinctive features of post-growth 78–84
  growth-oriented 68, 78–84
  militant 83
  post-growth *see* post-growth organizations
  public institutions 68
  start-ups 68
original equipment manufacturers (OEMs) 58–9, 63
Oroza, E. 71, 143–4n1
Oslo Manual 24
Owen, R. 43–4, 45
ownership and governance 78
ownership rights 60
ownership structures 72, 81–2, 87

P

P2P Lab 73, 80, 83
Palestine 29–30, 142n8
Pansera, M. 97, 98
Parker, M. 67
patent monopolies 127
People's Science Movement 70
Perez, C. 21, 118, 120
Período Especial 143n1(ch4)
physical extermination 29
physical layer (internet) 104–5, 107
Piketty, T. 82
Pinochet, A. 140n3(ch1)
Piscina Mirabilis 49–50, 65
planned obsolescence 53, 58, 64, 71
plastics 44
platform capitalism 76
platform cooperativism 109

playground communism 136
Polanyi, K. 80
political miracle 5
polycentric model of urban development 97
positive trends 24, 26
post growth 3, 6, 8, 9–10, 40
  framework 11
  future 7–8
  policy proposals 34
  position 3
  role of science, technology, and innovation 33–4
  see also degrowth
post-automation 109
post-growth innovation, implications for 63–6
post-growth organizations
  core values 78–80
  distinctive features 78–84
  examples 69–77
  governance structures 81–2
  intellectual property 83
  ownership structures 81–2
  resources 80–1
  scale of operation 84
  surplus management 82
  towards new approach to studies 85–7
poverty 42, 43
power relationships 79
private automobiles 36–7
privatization 80
productivism 11, 31, 35, 41–3, 45, 46, 134, 135
Prospera (ERC-funded project) 74
PROSPERA project 12
public transportation systems 37
publicly governed infrastructures 99

R

R2R movement *see* right-to-repair (R2R) movement
radical imaginary 139–40n3
Railcoop 77

rationalization 135
rebound effect 3
regional autonomy 97–8
regional scale 97–8
religion of economic growth 10
relocalization 127
renewable energy 2, 3, 24, 37, 77, 96, 121, 125
repair
  barriers to 53
  communitarian frame 61
  consumer rights frame 60
  as democratic struggle 63–4
  environmental frame 60
  grassroots innovation frame 60–1
  politics of 56–7, 63–4
  R2R movement *see* right-to-repair (R2R) movement
  right not to repair 64, 66
  workshops 127
replication of models 84, 97
research priorities 131–2
resource exhaustion 18
resource extraction 28–9
resource scarcity 107
responsible innovation 45
Rete Italiana delle Imprese Recuperate project 145n8
right-to-repair (R2R) movement 11, 58–63, 71, 115, 129, 130
  as democratic struggle 63–6
  EU Directive 62
  frames 60–1
  United States legislation 62
RiMaflow 124–5, 145n9
Romano, O. 82
Rosa, H. 14
rural educators 39
Russell, A. 21, 51, 52, 65

S

sacrifice zones 109
Savini, F. 97–8
scale, question of 94–9
scaling 79, 84, 87
Schumacher, F. 6, 46–7, 70
Schumpeter, J. 11, 16, 17, 24, 37–8, 54, 141n5
science, role of 33–4
Science and Technology Studies (STS) 35, 93, 95–6, 110, 128
Science Policy Research Unit (SPRU) 18, 19, 20
self-management system 124, 138
self-production initiatives 127
semiconductor industries 29
Serres, M. 96
Shelley, M. 55
Shove, E. 94
Silicon Valley elites 111, 112
simplicity and complexity 90
slow computing 109
small and medium-sized enterprises 114
small-scale enterprises 127
small-scale experiments 95
small-scale technologies 95, 96, 98
sober internet scenario 108–9
social agricultural cooperatives 84
social construction of infrastructure 92–4
social cooperatives 72, 97
social emancipation 83, 84
social movements 130, 133
Social Technology Network (STN) 71, 72, 82
socialist economies 32
socially useful production 6, 122
sociotechnical landscapes 100–1
sociotechnical systems 95–6
solidarity economy 72
Solow, R. 17–18
Som Energia 37
Soper, K. 6
space race 35–6, 86
Spain 13, 86
speculative ethics 56
'stack' (internet) 104, 108
stakeholder engagement 118
Star, S. L. 50
Starmer, K. 13
start-up state model 29

INDEX

state intervention 119
Stirling, A. 45
stock market 14
Strand, R. 31
strategic thinking 127–8
submarine cables 104–7, 109
subversive rationalization 116
supply chains 26, 89
surplus utilization 79, 82
sustainability 45, 47, 60, 62, 72, 73, 85, 119, 130
sustainable development 11, 20, 21
Swedish Central Bank 140n3(ch1)

T

technocratic governance 116
techno-fascism 145n2
technological change
  inevitability myth 35–6
  multiple pathways 36–7, 40–1
technological citizenship 59
technological determinism 11, 31, 35–41, 45, 46, 89, 115, 134, 135, 3541
technological disobedience 71
technological innovation 14, 23
technological momentum 103
technological optimism 15
technological progress, linear path myth 38
technological somnambulism 14, 103
technological sovereignty 127
Technologies for Social Inclusion movement 70
technology/technologies
  accountability for 55
  appropriate *see* appropriate technology
  care for 54–6
  democratizing 114–17, 129
  and designer values 93
  fragility of 52
  'loving our monsters' 55, 64
  and scale 94–9
  social meaning and functional rationality 135
  systems approach to 89–90
  undemocratic practices 113
techno-optimism 10–11
technopolitics 109
Trade in Services Agreement 83
trade unions 67, 113, 123, 125
Transatlantic Trade and Investment Partnership 83
transportation 110
Trentmann, F. 94
triple helix model 16
Trogal, T. 56
Trump, D. 13, 111, 112, 142n9

U

Uber 87
Ukraine 14
undemocratic practices
  acceptance of 113
  resistance to 116
underpinning resources 78
underpinning values 78
unemployment 42, 43
ungoverned innovation 43–4
unintended consequences, of innovation 43–4
union bargaining power, decline of 82
Unit 8200 29
United States 112, 118
  R2R legislation 62
  space race 35
universal basic income 128
universal basic services 128
universities 86, 113, 116
University of Sussex 18–19
urban technology, and politics 93
urbanization 139n2
USSR 32, 35–6

V

value creation 86
value-orientation 6
Vetter, A. 98, 128

Vienna Declaration 20
Viera Gallo, J. A. 88
Vinck, D. 117, 136
Vinsel, L. 21, 51, 52, 65
vitality-oriented economies 85

W

washing machines 137
waste colonies 53
water supply 110
Weber, M. 117
Weisman, A. 51–2
Wengrow, D. 116
Western industrial technologies 69
Western superiority, discourse of 112
Whig history 39, 142n2
Wikipedia 74, 98
Winner, L. 14, 40, 92–3, 103
women, care burden 57
worker cooperatives
 see cooperatives
worker-owned firms 12
worker-owned models 81
working class 32
working-time reduction 128
workplace democracy 86, 127
work-time reduction 86
World Business Council for Sustainable Development (WBCSD) 21, 141n4
World War II, post- 15–17
World3 model 19

X

X-Innovation 23

Y

Yoshihiro, N. 120
Yugoslavia 138

Printed and bound by CPI Group (UK) Ltd, Croydon, CR0 4YY

25/02/2026

14833373-0001